Mid-Atlantic
ROADSIDE DELIGHTS

To Joe Manning,
All the best!

Will Anderson

Peek a boo. I see you.
Four-year old Jonathan Buchwalter steals a look
from inside the "Historic" Village Diner.

Red Hook, New York
June, 1990

Roadside Architecture of Yesterday
And Today In New York, New Jersey, And Pennsylvania

Mid-Atlantic
ROADSIDE DELIGHTS

by Will Anderson

Studio Photography by A. & J. DuBois Commercial Photography,
Lewiston, Maine
Field Photography by the Author

Anderson & Sons' Publishing Company
7 Bramhall Terrace
Portland, Maine 04103

Other Books by the Author
New England Roadside Delights, 1989

Library of Congress Catalogue Card Number 90-85283

Anderson, Will 1940-
1. Roadside Architecture   2. Mid-Atlantic

ISBN 0-9601056-4-6

Designed and typeset by PrintMedia, Portland, Maine
Color separations by Graphic Color Service, Fairfield, Maine
Printed by Spectrum Printing and Graphics, Lewiston, Maine
Bound by Service Book Bindery, Portland, Maine

Cover design: Mitchell Fernie, PrintMedia

Cover graphics, clockwise from upper left:
Circa 1955 postcard view, Trent Diner, Trenton, N.J.
August, 1990 photograph, Jule's Service Diner, Bolton Landing, N.Y.
Circa 1955 postcard view, Woodworth's Restaurant, Geneva, N.Y.
Circa 1950 postcard view, Kendall Tourist Camp, Silver Creek, N.Y.
August, 1990 photograph, carhop Darla Basom, Crabbs Tropical Treat, Hanover, Pa.

Table of Contents

Acknowledgements

**Many, many people were good enough to help me in the researching and writing of
MID-ATLANTIC ROADSIDE DELIGHTS. I'd like to especially thank:**

Andy Anderson, University of Louisville Photographic Archives, Louisville, Ky.   Annita Andrick, Erie County Historical Society, Erie, Pa.

Fred Arone, Dobbs Ferry, N.Y.   Martin Aurand, Carnegie Mellon Architecture Archives, Pittsburgh, Pa.

Alex Beattie, SUNY, Oswego, N.Y.   Marcus "Skip" Bennett, Hudson, N.Y.

Gloria Bishop, Portland, Maine   T. Robins Brown, Bergen County Historic Preservation, Hackensack, N.J.

Marie Bruni, Huntington Memorial Library, Oneonta, N.Y.   Don Bull, Stamford, Conn.

Brian A. Butko, West Mifflin, Pa.   Rhoda W. Canter, Library of Congress, Washington, D.C.

Donna Comella, *Courier-Gazette*, Newark, N.Y.   Gus Correa, D-K Diner, West Chester, Pa.

Larry Cultrera, Medford, Mass.   Doratha Cummings, Wellsboro Diner, Wellsboro, Pa.

Barbara A. Evans, Lewis County Historical Society, Lyons Falls, N.Y.   June B. Griffiths, Lehigh County Historical Society, Allentown, Pa.

Arline & Sam Harkins, "Historic" Village Diner, Red Hook, N.Y.   Marjory B. Hinman, Broome County Historical Society, Binghamton, N.Y.

Edith Hoelle, Gloucester County Historical Society, Woodbury, N.J.   Bud Hundenski, Coraopolis, Pa.

John S. Joy, The Historical Society of Schuylkill County, Pottsville, Pa.   Ann Kane, Monroe County Public Library, Stroudsburg, Pa.

Mary Ann Kane, Cortland County Historical Society, Cortland, N.Y.   Elsie M. Maddaus, Ballston Spa Public Library, Ballston Spa, N.Y.

Jane Mains, Westmoreland County Historical Society, Greensburg, Pa.   Don March, Mamaroneck Historical Society, Mamaroneck, N.Y.

Janie Mason, Greensburg Area Library, Greensburg, Pa.   Al Matthews, Nottingham, N.H.

Fanny L. McCallum, Atlantic Highlands Historical Society, Atlantic Highlands, N.J.   Bob McCord, New York City, N.Y.

Jack McDougall, Cranford, N.J.   Harry McLaughlin, *The York Dispatch*, York, Pa.

Vivian C. McLaughlin, Resource & Research Center for Beaver County, Beaver Falls, Pa.   Charles C. Miller, Baltimore, Md.

Darlene Miller, The Lackawanna Historical Society, Scranton, Pa.   Iris Nevins, Sussex, New Jersey

Carl Peterson, Case Library/Colgate University, Hamilton, N.Y.   Helen Heid Platner, Heid's of Liverpool, Liverpool, N.Y.

Ronda Pollock, Portville Historical & Preservation Society, Portville, N.Y.   Pamela Powell, Chester County Historical Society, West Chester, Pa.

Charles L. Radzinsky, Middletown, N.Y.   Jerry Reed, Jerry's Curb Service, West Bridgewater, Pa.

Particia Robak, Oliver House Museum, Penn Yan, N.Y.   Eleanor Schnoor, North Castle Historical Society, Armonk, N.Y.

Blair Sandri, Lloyd's of Lowville, Lowville, N.Y.   Judith Seavey, Saco, Maine

Mary Shelley, Ithaca, N.Y.   Rick Stefanon, Silver Lake Drive-In Theatre, Perry, N.Y.

Joseph G. Streamer, Town Historian, Hamburg, N.Y.   Kay Vasiliades, Famous Lunch, Troy, N.Y.

John Walker, Pottsville Free Public Library, Pottsville, Pa.   Bob Weirich, Robesonia, Pa.

Willard B. Williams, Camillus, N.Y.   Daniel Zilka, American Diner Project, Burlington, Vt.

S.P. Ward, Lyme, Conn.   Austin Ward-Dienst, Lyme, Conn.   Gene Warrington, Walter's, Mamaroneck, N.Y.

Special Thanks To

long-time friend Jim Starkman of Fairport, New York for acting as advance scout and host in central/western New York, and to
Dianna Jean Montague and Kim Barry, both of PrintMedia, for their quite remarkable care and patience.

Special, Special Thanks To

good friends Tom, Alice, Vic, and Bob Hug, of Lorain, Ohio, for the exceedingly generous use of postcards and matchbook covers from their
most impressive collection of Advertising Americana.

Preface

MID-ATLANTIC ROADSIDE DELIGHTS is dedicated to all those who, in the rush toward the future, do not forget the wonder of the past.

In the beginning there was no automobile.

Then there was.

With it came the gas/filling/service station, the cabin court/motor court/motel, the drive-in/auto theatre, and a host of various and diverse eating establishments.

Beauty.

And beauty. Yes, beauty. More than a fair share of the roadside architecture of its Golden Era - 1920-1960 - is most definitely beautiful. Not beautiful like a waterfall or a village green, but beautiful like gleaming enamel, deco design, and colors bright.

Historic, too

Roadside architecture is historic, too. Historic not in the traditional sense - of a building where an armistice was signed or a battlefield where a major victory took place - but historic in that it represents a style, a period. There are a number of roadside structures in the Northeast already on the National Register of Historic Places. There deserve to be more.

Necessitates Care and Concern

It would be nice to be able to just highlight that roadside architecture can be beautiful, and historic, and then go out and order a double cheeseburger (rare, please, and hold the ketchup) to celebrate. But the plain and powerfully simple truth is that far too much of our roadside architecture is considered - both by the "average" person and historical preservationists as well - to be "throwaway"; use it, abuse it...and then tear it down and replace it with a newer model. So it's a fragile beauty, this roadside architecture of ours. A beauty that necessitates care and concern.

Mid-Atlantic Treasure Trove

New York, New Jersey, and Pennsylvania are fortunate to have had - and still to have - some of the very finest roadside architecture in America. Diners, cabin courts, drive-in theatres and restaurants...they're all here. ROADSIDE DELIGHTS celebrates this treasure trove. I've very much enjoyed researching and writing it. I very much hope that you enjoy reading it.

Will Anderson

In Three Parts

MID-ATLANTIC ROADSIDE DELIGHTS is divided into three parts. The first is an historical overview of roadside's "Big Five": the diner, the gas station, the cabin court/motel, the drive-in restaurant, and the drive-in theatre. Second is a scrapbook featuring some of the region's more memorable 1920-1960 roadside views. It's meant to put you in a yesteryear frame of mind. Third is a visit - although "tribute" would perhaps be a more fitting word - to a hefty sampling of the most attractive and most intriguing of the region's present-day roadside structures. It is the book's longest section. It deserves to be: there are some wonderful places out there.

Believe It Or Not

It's sometimes difficult to believe, but gas stations, diners, drive-in restaurants and theatres, cabin courts and motels haven't been around forever. All are developments of this century. All evolved to serve the needs and wants of the motorist and his/her passengers. All have had a profound influence on our culture, our lifestyles.

KENDALL TOURIST CAMP — 1½ MILES WEST OF SILVER CREEK. N. Y.

MOTOR ROUTE U. S. 20 — PHONE SILVER CREEK 40-J   61098

Circa 1940 postcard view.

Hand In Hand

The Automobile and Roadside Architecture

Roadside Architecture: An Overview

Taken literally, "roadside" means anything - and everything - that one might see along the road: houses, telephone poles, trees, etc., etc. The term, however, has basically come to mean "that which was created to serve the motorist." Following, in more or less chronological sequence, is a look at each of the major facets of roadside architecture: structures created to serve the motorist. Omitted are several categories that could have been included -

billboards and auto showrooms and curio/souvenir shops prominent among them - in order to be able to better concentrate on the Big Five: the diner, the gas station, the motel, the drive-in restaurant, and the drive-in theatre. In addition, there's a glimpse at the evolution of those two phenomena that have come to so dominate our present-day roadside horizon: the family restaurant, and the chain.

Here Comes The Automobile

The automobile was not a revered species when it evolved on the scene in the last decade of the 1890s and the wee years of this century. "Reviled" might, in fact, have been a more apt word. It made noise, created dust and pollution and confusion, scared horses and farmers' animals half to death, and , for that matter, scared the farmers - and other folks - half to death, too.

But the automobile, for all its negatives, had its fascination. Very strong fascination. It spelled mobility and freedom. Freedom to come and go as one chose, rather than having to rely on train or trolley schedules. And in far more comfort than had ever before been possible.

So it's no wonder that the automobile caught on. What is perhaps

First Pedestrian : Well, I am afraid that automobile is gone for good.
Second Ped.: Yes.   But I am very much afraid he will still be able to use another.

Auto Fun

These cartoon sketches, all from a 1905 book entitled AUTO FUN *(New York: Thomas Y. Crowell & Co.), poke fun at how a goodly share of the populace viewed the automobile in its earliest years. But it wasn't all fun and cartoons. Sunset magazine reported villages in which "some four-mile-an-hour law" was rigidly enforced; others where ropes were strung across the main thoroughfares or low mounds were constructed with "the intention of smashing your springs" if you proceeded over them at anything but a crawl. Pretty serious stuff.*

No, America's love affair with the auto began more like a lovers' quarrel. But once it began to blossom, watch out... there was no stopping it!

Paderewsky Making a Tour in His Pianomobile.

"Now, old chap, you'll have a chance to enjoy the sweet odors emitted by your own machine."

"Hey, Mister! You dropped your hat."

worthy of wonder, however, is the speed with which it caught on. In 1900 there were a scant 8,000 "horseless carriages" registered on the American road. By 1910 that number had risen to 458,300. And by 1920 the count was a rather colossal 8,131,500. The automobile was here to stay. And to perhaps change how we live more than any other single creation in the history of mankind.

SEEING THE SIGHTS

"Look, Maria! There goes one of them automobiles! Shall we hail the thing and take a ride?"

The Eat-a-Bite Wheel Cafe, Potsdam, New York, Circa 1900.

To attract attention, many an early lunch wagon was done up in fancy-even florid-designs, often complete with stained glass windows. A fine example, indeed, was Potsdam's Eat-a-Bite, shown with proprietor Benjamin Miles at the dawn of the century.

Roadside's "Senior Citizen"

The Diner

The diner - or its roots, anyway - actually predate the automobile. In 1872, one Walter Scott, of Providence, Rhode Island, noticed that if you wanted a square meal around town after the sun went down you were basically out of luck. About your only choice was the neighborhood saloon. That, and your own kitchen.

Walter set out to remedy the situation. He took a horse-drawn wagon, cut holes on both sides, whipped up a sizable array of sandwiches, pies, and steaming hot coffee, and positioned his wagon full of goodies beside Journal Square, directly across from the *Providence Journal.* He reasoned that he'd get the night-time trade of the newspaper crews as they came off shift. And he did. But he got a whole lot more,

too: policemen, after-theatre goers, and just plain late night revelers. They all lined up outside Walter Scott's wagon. And he fed them all through his cut-out windows.

Success, of course, seldom goes unnoticed... and by the early 1880s there were thirty such carts in operation in Providence alone.

Enter Worcester

Providence may have given birth to it, but it was Worcester, Massachusetts that really ran with the diner. First came Sam Jones: he took Walter Scott's idea and literally enlarged upon it, creating a wagon - in 1887 - spacious enough for patrons to come inside, rather than having to wait outside. Next came another Worcesterite, Charles Palmer, with the vision to

project the success of the lunch wagon beyond the confines of southeastern New England: he began a lunch wagon manufacturing company. That was in 1891. Yet another Worcesterite, one Thomas H. Buckley, topped them all by not only producing, but *mass producing,* the lunch wagon. His firm, the New England Lunch Wagon Company (later the T.H. Buckley Lunch Wagon Manufacturing and Catering Company), churned out hundreds of built-in-Worcester wagons in the 1890s and the better part of the first decade of this century. And last, another firm, the Worcester Lunch Car Company, was one of the nation's pre-eminent diner manufacturing companies for all of its fifty-six years of operation, beginning in 1906 and continuing on until 1962.

continued on page 11

"Diner": The Origin of the Word
The term "diner" (as in a place to eat, as opposed to one who eats) came into usage in the mid-1920s. Its derivation was basic: from Walter Scott's humble creation this was a structure that had increasingly come to resemble a railroad dining car.

In Providence - where it had all begun - "diner" made its first appearance in 1926. In that year the city's business directory listed both the Checker Diner and the Ever Ready Diner.
It was a term that would endure.

Circa 1900 T.H. Buckley White House Cafe, location
unknown

Thomas H. Buckley: Quite A Guy

By all accounts, Thomas H. Buckley was quite a guy. As a visionary, he foresaw lunch wagons in every sizable community in America. In fact, if such a community did not have a wagon, Buckley would appear before the town council to put forth the merits of why it should. He would sell wagons or he would lease them. By 1900, it is estimated that he had one or more of his wagons in 275 American cities. As a prohibitionist, he produced a wagon he christened the Way-Side Inn for use by temperance societies in New York City and elsewhere. The idea: to serve a good meal for such a low price that the wayward-prone would be less tempted to partake of the free lunch - washed down, no doubt, with an alcoholic beverage or two - offered up by the saloons of the day. As a manufacturer, he was a craftsman. He developed six models - each, with the exception of the Way-Side Inn, named White House Cafe -and each respected for its beauty. Stained glass windows, fanciful scrolls and lettering ... all were featured in Buckley's lovely-to-look-at creations.

Alas, however, Thomas H. Buckley died at the young age of 35, in 1903. Shortly thereafter the company that bore his name appears to have shifted its emphasis to the manufacture of automobiles. It was to prove a mistake: by 1909, the company was out of business.

Established 1889.   Incorporated 1897.

THE
T. H. BUCKLEY LUNCH WAGON MANUFACTURING AND CATERING COMPANY.

Night Lunch Wagons of Every Description

FOR SALE OR TO LET.

Builders and Designers of

"White House Cafe" Lunch Wagons, "The Best Made."
TRADE MARK.

Also Builders and Operators of "Kiosk" Quick Lunch Cafés.

Factory and Facilities second to none.

Office and Factory: Rear No. 281 Grafton Street.
WORCESTER, MASS.

WORCESTER DIRECTORY ad, 1903

WORCESTER DIRECTORY ad, 1906

The T. H. Buckley Car Mfg. Co., JOHN T. FLANAGAN, Pres. and Treas. CHAS. A. LEGGE, Vice-Pres.

ELECTRIC AND STEAM CARS, also Designers and Builders of WHITE HOUSE CAFE LUNCH WAGONS, Patented

Office and Factory: 281 GRAFTON STREET, Worcester, Mass.

Take Your Pick
     Everybody likes diners...and for a host of good reasons. See if you can find your favorite reason(s) among this treasure trove of Mid-Atlantic diner ads from days gone by.

IT'S A TREAT TO EAT

at the

MATAMORAS DINER

TOMMY FIELDING, Prop.

Penna. Ave.

"It's A Treat To Eat"
Matamoras Diner,
Matamoras, Pa., 1940

Just a Good Place to Eat

109½ E. Dominick St.

National Diner

ROBERT McKEAN, Mgr.

"Just a Good Place to Eat"
National Diner, Rome, N.Y., 1934

Queensborough Lunch

Business Men's Delight

The Goods Are Right and Cooked in Sight
C. Morenus, Prop.

41 S. MAIN ST.,

GLOVERSVILLE, N. Y.

"Cooked in Sight"
Queensborough Lunch,
Gloversville, N.Y., 1916

"THE PLACE TO MEET IS THE PLACE TO EAT"

AT

THE SQUIRE DINER

Most modern and pleasant establishment in West Chester

Fully Air-Conditioned and the Finest of Food Anywhere

305 E. GAY STREET
West Chester ,Pa.

"Fully Air-Conditioned"
Squire Diner,
West Chester, Pa., 1953

"Good Food at
Reasonable Prices"
People's Diner,
Montrose, Pa., 1960

PEOPLE'S DINER

Good Food IS NOT CHEAP,

Cheap Food IS NOT GOOD

We Serve Good Food at Reasonable Prices

Mary and Mike Knopick

Public Ave.   Montrose, Pa.

POTTER'S DINER and MOTEL
HOME OF GOOD FOOD
OPEN 24 HOURS

JUST THE PLACE FOR A GOOD MEAL OR A SNACK

South End of Village
Route 9, Warrensburg   Tel. NA 3-9889

"Open 24 Hours"
Potter's Diner and Motel,
Warrensburg, N.Y., 1962

SMITTY'S DINER

23 Groton Ave.   Phone 2234

Good home cooked food. Meet your
friends here. Thank you

"Good home cooked food"
Smitty's Diner,
Cortland, N.Y., 1942

DIXIE DINER
The Place to Meet and Eat
Air Cooled
Route 17   Middletown, N. Y.

"The Place to Meet and Eat"
Dixie Diner, Middletown, N.Y., 1939

RHINEBECK DINER

Rhinebeck, N. Y., on Route 9
Largest and Most Modern Diner
in the State
Nothing but Best Food Obtainable
Served
Cleanliness is Our Motto
Montreal-New York Bus-Stop

T. Djines, Proprietor   Phone 381

"Nothing but Best Food Obtainable Served"
Rhinebeck Diner, Rhinebeck, N.Y., 1939

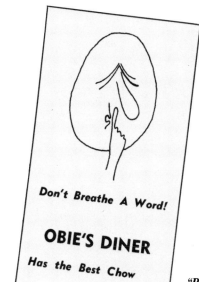

Don't Breathe A Word!

OBIE'S DINER

Has the Best Chow
In Ithaca

1016 W. STATE

"Best Chow"
Obie's Diner,
Ithaca, N.Y., 1958

𝔐𝔦𝔰𝔰 𝔓𝔩𝔞𝔱𝔱𝔰𝔟𝔲𝔯𝔤
𝔇𝔦𝔫𝔢𝔯

13 Protection Ave.

Open day and night

Best coffee in the city

Regular Dinners 50c

"Best coffee in the city"
Miss Plattsburg Diner,
Plattsburgh, N.Y., 1931

Next to Home This is the
BEST PLACE TO EAT

MILFORD DINER

Milford, Pa.

Next to Home This is the Best Place To Eat"
Milford Diner, Milford, Pa., 1938

"One of the World's Finest and Best Equipped Diners"
ROUTE 29 (Opposite Somerset Bus Terminal) Mountainside, N. J.
10 Miles Southwest of Newark Airport

Postcard views, circa 1950

A Pair of Garden State Beauties
    Although it was born in New England, it is New Jersey that has become perhaps most synonymous with diners in the mind of many. Here's a pair of beauties from the state that's manufactured more of 'em than any other.

1950 STATE HIGHWAY RT. 25, RAHWAY, N. J.

An All East Coast Line-Up

In spite of their many contributions, however, never let it be said that the diner is an all Providence/Worcester product. It can be said, however, that it has a virtually all east coast heritage. In addition to the Worcester Lunch Car Company, the country's leading diner manufacturers have consisted of the Fodero Dining Car Company (Bloomfield/Newark, New Jersey), the Kuhlman Dining Car Company (Harrison/Avenel, New Jersey), Mountain View Diners (Singac, New Jersey), Silk City Diners (Paterson Vehicle Company, Paterson, New Jersey), Paramount Diners (Haledon, New Jersey), Master Diners (Pequannock, New Jersey), De Raffele Diner Manufacturing Company (New Rochelle, New York), Jerry O'Mahony, Inc. (Bayonne/Elizabeth, New Jersey), Sterling Diners (J.B. Judkins Co.,

Merrimac, Massachusetts), and P.J. Tierney Sons Company (New Rochelle, New York).

The latter three - plus Worcester Lunch Car - are especially worthy of note: Jerry O'Mahony started out in a smallish garage in Bayonne in 1913 and rose to be the kingpin of his time; P.J. ("Pop") Tierney would go to almost any length to get someone to set up a lunch wagon (preferably one of his, of course!) and by 1925 the firm he'd founded was turning out a diner a day; Sterling produced some of the sleekest diners this side of Art Deco in the 1930s and 1940s (you'd almost wager your paycheck that a Sterling Streamliner was in reality the 20th Century Limited, about to take off for Chicago and other points west); Worcester Lunch Car will always be remembered for its wonderfully colorful and beautiful porcelainized metal facades (and for the durability of its diners: its unofficial slogan: "In New Jersey they've got class, but we build them to last.")

Give It a Try...and Enjoy

From a peak of 6,000 or so in the 1940s, the count of true diners (to be a "true" diner, by diner buff standards, the structure must have been prefabricated: converted stores, garages, etc. don't count) has shrunk to perhaps a tenth of that number. Fast food franchising has not been kind to diners.

Fortunately, however, there has been and continues to be a rekindled appreciation of diners...not just as settings for movies and television ads, but as places in which to eat. To bring friends and/or the family. To enjoy a good fixed-right-there meal at an easy-on-the-budget price.

Give it a try... and enjoy.

"The laziest lunch-wagon man in Rome is the one who puts popcorn in his pancakes so they'll turn over by themselves."

Joke, **Souvenir Program for the Fifth Annual Dance, Police Benevolent Association, Rome, New York,** April 27, 1934.

It's Come Full Circle

The Gas Station

America didn't just wake up one morning to find itself gazing into the eyes of the gas station. No, the gas station evolved over decades. Several decades.

Gas was initially sold, strictly as a sideline, by a number of outlets: general stores, hardware stores, grocery stores, pharmacies, blacksmith shops. (Actually, until the advent of the internal combustion engine and the automobile in the 1890s, gasoline wasn't sold by anybody: as refiners processed kerosene from crude petroleum there was also produced gasoline, an explosive and dangerous by-product that nobody wanted. It was disposed of as quickly as possible, either by dumping or burning it off). You bought it by the canful, much as you might buy coffee or maple syrup. The gas pump, introduced in 1905, changed all that. Initially pumps, however, were largely the province of the same general store, drug store et al bevy that had been selling it by the canful. Their pumps - or, more likely, pump - were curbside...which was fine and dandy until ever-increasing automobile sales lead to ever-increasing curbside business which lead, not surprisingly, to traffic jams.

To avert this curbside congestion - and to gain greater control over the marketing of their products - the larger petroleum companies began to construct their own edifices solely for the sale of gas and oil and related products. The Automobile Gasoline Company built a small chain of such structures in St. Louis starting in 1905. Standard Oil opened its first, in Seattle, in 1907, with the Texas Company (Texaco) following suit in 1911. And by World War I such edifices - generally always constructed with the pumps set back from the curb - were appearing at the rate of well over a thousand a year. The gas station had arrived.

At first, quantity definitely appeared to count for far more than quality: stations were hastily constructed, bordering on the ramshackle. By the 1920s, however, a combination of corporate pride plus fear of civic scorn lead the major petroleum firms to begin to build aesthetics into their stations. Some stations, generally within larger city limits, were modeled after the monumental. Thus we had stations in the form of miniature banks, libraries, city halls, etc. A cartoon of the time shows a man, pointing at a noticeably majestic edifice, exclaiming "I didn't know that the State Capitol was located in this town." Guffaws his companion, "Haw! Haw! Haw! State Capitol your eye! That's our latest gas station!"

continued on page 16

Touting the benefits of Hi-Speed Lubrication: circa 1940 matchbook cover art

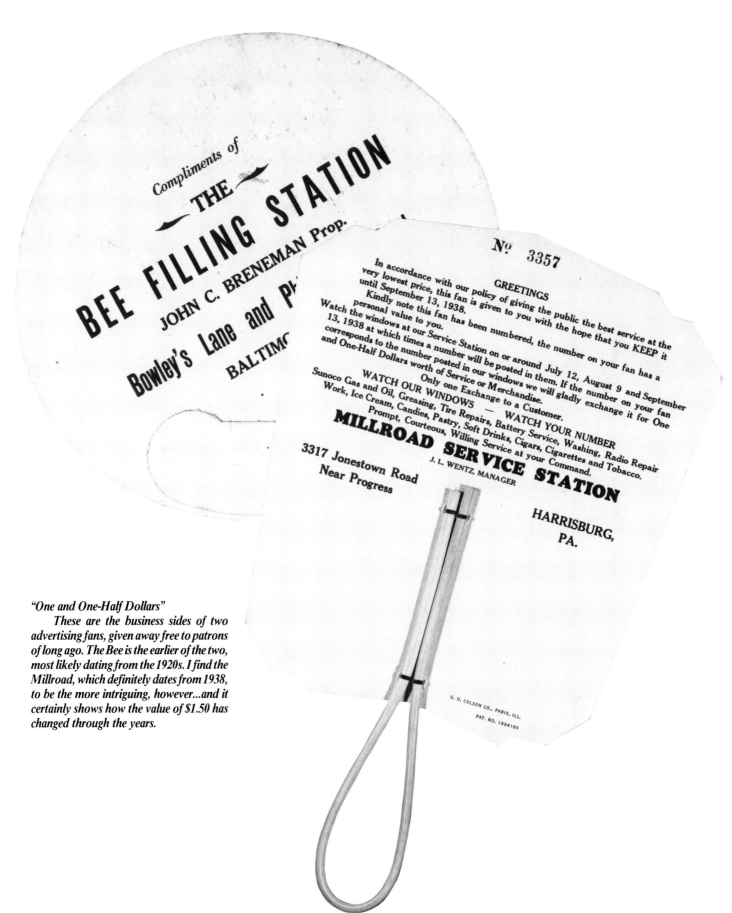

Compliments of
THE
BEE FILLING STATION
JOHN C. BRENEMAN Prop.
Bowley's Lane and P
BALTIMO

N⁰ 3357

GREETINGS

In accordance with our policy of giving the public the best service at the very lowest price, this fan is given to you with the hope that you KEEP it until September 13, 1938.

Kindly note this fan has been numbered, the number on your fan has a personal value to you.

Watch the windows at our Service Station on or around July 12, August 9 and September 13, 1938 at which times a number will be posted in them. If the number on your fan corresponds to the number posted in our windows we will gladly exchange it for One and One-Half Dollars worth of Service or Merchandise.

Only one Exchange to a Customer.

WATCH OUR WINDOWS — WATCH YOUR NUMBER

Sunoco Gas and Oil, Greasing, Tire Repairs, Battery Service, Washing, Radio Repair Work, Ice Cream, Candies, Pastry, Soft Drinks, Cigars, Cigarettes and Tobacco.

Prompt, Courteous, Willing Service at your Command.

MILLROAD SERVICE STATION

J. L. WENTZ, MANAGER

3317 Jonestown Road
Near Progress

HARRISBURG,
PA.

U. O. COLSON CO., PARIS, ILL.
PAT. NO. 1994105

"One and One-Half Dollars"

These are the business sides of two advertising fans, given away free to patrons of long ago. The Bee is the earlier of the two, most likely dating from the 1920s. I find the Millroad, which definitely dates from 1938, to be the more intriguing, however...and it certainly shows how the value of $1.50 has changed through the years.

The Road Map as a Thing of Beauty

Up until less than a decade and a half ago part of the "service" provided by service stations was free road maps. It was Gulf that started the practice of gratis maps - in 1914 - in the hope, undoubtedly, that it would lead to increased sales of their "Good Gulf" gasoline. Not only were they free, but road maps from decades gone by were often strikingly beautiful. Here's a mini-collection of Mid-Atlantic 1920s' and 1930s' lovelies.

"Take Care...and Buy Sinclair"
  Sinclair - noted for its irresistible Dino the Dinosaur symbol - had a claim to map fame as well. Its 1930s' maps always seemed to unfold into the most wonderful of pana-ramas. Here is a pair of my favorites.

Another joke tells of a man from the midwest who, upon seeing Grant's Tomb, stops his car and beckens to the guard to "fill 'er up."

Most stations, of course, were far less elaborate. They were, however, designed to appear neat and tidy, very often taking the shape of a small bungalow or house. And, like as not, a small bungalow or house that featured a canopy - or porte cochère - extending out over the pumps to shelter customers and attendants in the event of inclement weather. Most were prefabricated: selected from the manufacturer's catalogue, they could be set up and ready to operate in almost no time flat.

By the 1930s, however, the gas - or filling - station was evolving into a place to do more than just purchase gas and oil. Up until that time, most auto servicing was performed at a garage or in a car dealer's shop. Increasingly, though, these facilities were not able to keep up. There were simply too many cars on the road that needed to be cared for. The cute little bungalow or house design was no longer adequate.

A new design - one that allowed for the efficient addition of service bays and the display of tires and parts for sale - was called for. It arrived in the form of "the box." While there were a number of variations, from company to company and/or depending on site layout, the basic box was designed to provide not only adequate space for

September, 1990 photograph

Classic box design station, Bernie's Service Center, Route 9, New Gretna, New Jersey

16

The White Patrol

While Gulf began the long-standing tradition of gratis road maps, it was Texaco that pioneered the promotion of clean rest rooms. They were not only clean, they were "Registered." As explained in the Texas Company's spring, 1938 advertising:

"A new kind of rest room is now appearing by the thousands...along America's highways everywhere...'Registered' Rest Rooms!

Rest rooms that are regularly kept clean and fully supplied, with running water, soap, towels and mirror for your convenience.

Rest rooms that are individually numbered and registered for your protection. And marked at thousands of Texaco Dealers' stations by the neat green-and-white sign at the curb."

And, so you knew they weren't just whistling Dixie, Texaco maintained a fleet of "White Patrol" cars. Manned by "trained inspectors," the White Patrol was on the road in all forty-eight states to ensure that every Registered Rest Room lived up to its neat and tidy billing.

Texaco Registered Rest Rooms ad, 1938

sales and service but to be quite sleek in appearance as well. Reflecting the Streamline Moderne look then coming into vogue, box stations were generally white or light pastel. Thin lines or bands, akin to pinstripes, often adorned the upper facade, which was apt to be gleaming enamel-over-metal. All in all, the box-style service station did its designers proud. And the better part of two generations of Americans - from the 1930s until the mid-1950s - grew up with it as their conception of what a service station was all about.

In the past four decades or so we've come, in many ways, full tilt. The self-service concept - begun in California in 1947 - has lead the swing away from the service station back to the gas station...with the primary building being either a shed-like (i.e., bungalow-like throwback to the days of the 1920s) affair for the pump starter/money collector or a fairly large-scale store, with sales of a little bit of everything (which, of course, is strangely reminiscent of the station's very beginnings). Sometimes, as goes the old adage, the more things change the more they stay the same.

A Room For A Night

Auto Camps and Cabin Courts and Motels

The motel is certainly the least glamorous of roadside's several categories. Yet roadside lodging has run the gamut from cabin villages to tepees to reproductions of Mount Vernon and the Alamo. And motel postcards are often exceedingly colorful.

In the pioneer days of motoring, ones choice of lodging while on the road was slim. The options quickly narrowed down to heading for a city or town populous enough to have a hotel, or to finding a place along the road and camping out. Both had their pitfalls.

With the hotel there was the hauling in - to a room that always seemed to be upstairs - and the hauling out of luggage. With the camp-out you were squarely at the mercy of the elements, such wild animals/insects as might decide to keep you company, and/or a property-owner who didn't care for you on his/her property.

The first accommodations designed with the motorist in mind was the auto camp. An auto camp was an area set aside for motorists and their cars: the motorist supplied a tent, the camp

provided space. At first, in the years just preceeding World War I and into the early 1920s, the vast majority of America's auto camps were operated free of charge by various and diverse municipalities. The thinking was simple: during their stay in Our Town the motorists and their families are likely to patronize Our Town's cafes, stores, and other shopping facilities.

While most of these municipal auto camps were small, and Spartan at best, there were those that almost bordered on the elaborate. Denver's

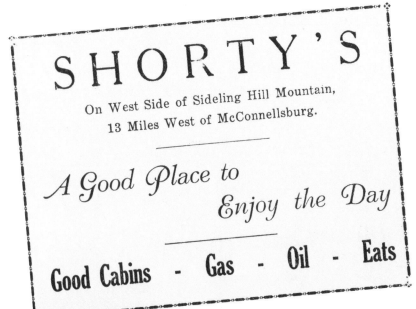

Who Could Ask For Anything More?
Shorty's Good Cabins-Gas-Oil-Eats
ad, McConnellsburg, Pa., 1930

Motor City was perhaps the most grandiose of all. Opened in 1918, Motor City devoted sixty acres to the camp. There were coin-operated cooking facilities, comfort stations, tennis courts, and a lake stocked with black bass. There was even a playground complete with swings, teeter-totters, a merry-go-round and, as so nicely phrased by *Motor* magazine, "other features designed to delight the susceptible heart of childhood."

Such idyllic - and gratis - settings were not, however, to last long. By the mid-twenties a tremendous surge in auto tourism lead to camps that were just plain overcrowded. Many municipalities, meanwhile, were coming to the conclusion that the camps were drawing "undesirables" to their fair communities. To combat both problems they started to charge a fee for camping. Private facilities, now that there was a chance to make money, began to appear. And their proprietors were not long in discovering that the more that was provided the higher the fee could be. Motorists liked comfort, and were willing to pay for it.

Improved sanitary facilities, pre-pitched tents, even little cabins...all began to dot the motorist landscape. And all were accepted with enthusiasm and an open wallet. By the late 1920s, auto tourist accommodations were fast becoming quite comfortable, if not downright luxurious. Cabin courts, parading neat rows or semi-circles of cabins, graced the outskirts of most all towns of consequence. Now a motorist not only had a parking spot for the night, he/she had his/her own little house as well. Often adorned with shutters, flower boxes and/or similar embellishments on the outside, the cabin's inside was likely to offer comforts heretofore reserved for hotel/inn guests: real beds with real mat-tresses, tables and chairs, a closet area, sink with running water, etc. Perhaps even a radio.

As cozy as they were - and are: many cabin complexes yet serve the traveling public - cabins eventually gave way to what we now call the "motel." Although other terms were experimented with -"tourotel" is one that had a following for a time - "motel" is the one that has stuck. A marriage of "motor" and "hotel," the term was initially used in 1925 in southern California. It gained ever-increasingly in favor as auto travel boomed in the post-World War II years, the same period of time that saw single-unit construction become the norm for highway lodging. Prospective motel hosts discovered that erecting one long or L-shaped structure was less costly than erecting a string of cabins, and easier to maintain, too.

1940s' matchcover art

Circa 1940 cabin court postcard views

FONDA'S CABINS AND RESTAURANT

U. S. ROUTE 20 - GUILDERLAND, N. Y.

The Famous BEAUTY SPOT

TROY, N. Y. — BENNINGTON, VT. ROAD — N. Y. ROUTE No. 7   7A-H2511

"All the Conveniences of Home"

The short message to the folks back home that was penned on the reverse of the Beauty Spot card said a lot about how far roadside lodging had progressed since the days of camping by the side of the road. Sent, on August 25, 1940, by a couple who were good enough to even mark off which cabin was theirs ("ours"), it read: "We have had a nice trip today. We are staying in a modern cabin with shower and everything. All the conveniences of home."

Where It All Happened

Main Street

What does Main Street have to do with roadside? It's a legitimate question. One almost seems the antithesis of the other. Yet, in reality, Main Street was roadside. In the twenties and thirties and even into the forties, if you were traveling from Town A to Town B, more than likely you ate in either Town, gassed up in either Town, obtained lodging in either Town. There

simply wasn't much in-between. Sure, on the fringes - the outskirts - there were places. And with each passing year there were more. That's what this book is about. Yet, chances are you still accomplished many of your on-the-road basics - gas, food, lodging - downtown. And it's for sure where you did any other shopping that might be

necessary: the shopping center/mall was a long way off.

So, yes, there are Main Street places - mostly restaurants - included in **MID-ATLANTIC ROADSIDE DELIGHTS**. And there's even a four-page spread of Main Street postcard views included. Right here. Main Street: it really is where it all happened.

LOOKING NORTH ON WYOMING AVE.. KINGSTON CORNERS. PA.

Main Street, Herkimer, N. Y.

6B557-N

Main Street postcard views, circa 1940s. While the cars and many of the stores, eating establishments et al have changed, the towns live on. And so does Main Street.

Ford Street Looking East, Ogdensburg, N. Y.

7A-H3302

Grand Central Avenue, Looking South, Lavallette, N. J.

High Street Looking North, Burlington, N. J.

Northampton Street, Looking West from Center Sq. Easton, Pa.

Main Street Looking West, Johnson City, N. Y.

EAST TIOGA STREET, TUNKHANNOCK, PA.

Third Street Looking West, Jamestown, N. Y.

Happy Seventieth Birthday

The Drive-In Restaurant

"Drive-in": it's become a mixed-up, muddled-up term insofar as restaurants are concerned. It used to mean curb or carhop service: you drove your Hudson or Hupmobile or Ford or whatever into the restaurant's lot, parked it, and were waited on while sitting in your car. Nowadays, however, a drive-in is much more apt to be just a place - in many cases a former "real" drive-in that yet retains its former name - where you drive your Honda or Saab or Ford or whatever into the lot, park it... but then get out, walk inside, and get served just like any traditional restaurant. Then, of course, there's the "drive-through"/"drive-thru" popularized by McDonald's, Burger King, Arby's, etc.

But let's be purists. Let's discuss only the drive-in-and-be-served-in-your-car drive-ins. With carhops that smile and trays that hook ever so neatly onto your window.

The first restaurant credited with being set up solely to serve customers in their vehicle was the Pig Stand, opened for business on the Dallas-Fort Worth Highway in September of 1921. The brainchild of Dallas candy and tobacco wholesaler J.G. Kirby - who once reputedly commented that "People with cars are so lazy they don't want to get out of them to go eat" - the Pig Stand was a success from its very start. A barbequed pork sandwich - the restaurant's namesake and specialty - savored

in the comfort of your car was a tough combination to beat! Within scarcely more than a decade there were over sixty Pig Stands serving customers across seven states. Competitors, too, joined the drive-in ranks. Restaurant and hotel veteran Roy W. Allen teamed up with Frank Wright in 1922 to open a trio of walk-up root beer stands in Houston under the name of A & W... "A" for Allen; "W" for Wright. The very next year they went one step further: they opened an A & W Drive-In, in Sacramento, California, at which "tray boys" did the walking: all the customer had to do was sit in his/her car and enjoy his/her ice-cold root beer.

Matchbook art from the 1940s.

Marbett's and its jauntily-attired curb service squadron, Camden, New Jersey, 1938.

Marbett's

In the late 1930s, White Towers (see pages 42-46) decided to experiment with going "full-fledged": their architect, Charles J. Johnson, designed a full-scale restaurant, set up for both eat-in and curb service. The name was different, too. The new deluxe model - with hamburgers for 10¢, rather than the Towers' norm of 5¢ - was called Marbett's, a snappy combination of Margaret and Betty, sisters of White Towers' founder T.E. Saxe. The first Marbett's swung into operation in Camden, New Jersey in 1938. Another full-scale model opened in Silver Spring, Maryland later the same year. Neither was to prove particularly successful, and White Towers' management would decide to stick with its traditional small units.

By a decade later, 1933, there were 171 A & W stands spread across America, mostly Midwest and far West America, and mostly on a franchised basis. Not all A & W franchisees, however, were "out west": J. Willard Marriott (as in today's Marriott hotel chain!) combined A & W's root beer with spicy Mexican food under the name "Hot Shoppe" in Washington, D.C. starting in 1927. As Philip Langdon writes in his excellent book, **ORANGE ROOFS, GOLDEN ARCHES** (New York City: Alfred A. Knopf, 1986), "By 1930, Marriott had branched out along the Washington area's major streets with a series of Hot Shoppes operating in routine rectangular (drive-in) buildings, but with roofs painted an eye-catching orange. Marriott and Howard Johnson were later to argue about whose orange roofs appeared first."

Great Depression or not, Pig Stands, A & W's, Hot Shoppes - plus many, many others - proliferated across the country in the 1930s. In fact, perhaps the drive-in restaurant's moment of greatest glory came when the February 26, 1940 issue of *Life* magazine sported comely carhop Josephine Powell, adorned in what would otherwise have passed for a majorette's outfit, on its front cover. Inside, in a wonderfully illustrated article entitled "Houston's Drive-In Trade Gets Girl Show With Its Hamburgers," *Life* focused on the happenings at Silvils' Drive-In on the outskirts of Houston. Opened for business less than a year earlier, Silvils' started with but five carhops (so named, legend has it, because of their penchant for hopping on the running boards of patron's cars... back when cars had running boards), but the five "curly-

On The Job At The Drive-In
While many drive-in proprietors favored female car hops, "tray boys" were far from unknown. Here's a pair on the job at Washington, D.C.-area Hot Shoppes in the early 1940s.

The Drive-In Restaurant

haired cuties...in abbreviated uniforms," as *Life* so picturesquely put it, soon increased to twenty-five and then fifty and, by the time of the magazine feature, to just short of a solid hundred. "Applicants," *Life* further reported, "must be between 18 and 25, have good figures, a high-school education, health cards and 'come-hither' personalities."

After a wartime lull - gas rationing had a way of putting a hold on all

businesses that were auto-related - the drive-in came back stronger than ever. America's move to Suburbia in the second half of the 1940s and early 1950s fueled roadside fare as never before: everyone had a car; everyone wanted to spend as much time in it as they could; drive-ins were only too happy to oblige.

Eventually, of course, fast food chains that served indoors and/or with

"drive-thru" service - thereby eliminating both the expense of carhops and the negative of seasonal weather variations - put a major dent in true curb service operations. But a dent is not a demise and, it's nice to be able to report, drive-in service lives on - especially in the summer, of course - throughout much of roadside America. "Lights on for service."

Carhopping It In 1940
Carhop Josephine Powell as she appeared on the cover of Life *in February of 1940. She and her sister carhops each had two uniforms, made of satin. They had to be kept spotless. Ditto with the boots, which had to be shined daily. Each girl worked a 45½-hour week, received no regular pay, but did get to keep any and all tips she took in. The average: $30.00 a week...not bad money five decades ago.*

LIFE

ROADSIDE SERVICE

FEBRUARY 26, 1940 **10** CENTS

The Drive-In Theatre Is Born
    The world's first drive-in theatre, on Admiral Wilson Boulevard in Camden, New Jersey, as it appeared in its inaugural month, June of 1933. It could accommodate five-hundred cars in nine rows and, according to its advertising, showed "abridged features, with all the dull or uninteresting parts omitted."

"Enjoy Movies In Your Car"

The Drive-In Movie Theatre

1930s' drive-in
movie theatre
advertising art

Richard M. Hollingshead, Jr. (1900-1975) was a man with a mission. The time was the early 1930s, the Great Depression was weighing heavy, and Hollingshead was out of work. But he had an idea he believed could be a winner: marry those two great American passions, the automobile and the movies, he reasoned, and people would come by the drove, Depression or no Depression.

After a period of experimentation with a projector and a screen in the front yard of his house in Riverton, New Jersey, Hollingshead and his

cousin, Willis W. Smith, formed Park-In Theatres, Inc...and proceeded to construct the world's first drive-in, which they named the Automobile Movie Theatre, on a ten-acre site on Crescent Boulevard (now Admiral Wilson Boulevard) in Camden. The Grand Opening was June 6, 1933, and an estimated six-hundred paying customers turned out for the history-making event. The price was 25¢ a car plus 25¢ a person, with a maximum of $1.00. The feature was a three-year old film entitled "Wife Beware," starring Adolphe Menjou.

The fact that Hollingshead's first feature was a dated one portended what was to be one of the drive-in's biggest problems: film distributors, partial to the established "hardtop" (as traditional indoor theatres were called in the trade) operators, were generally reluctant to offer first-rate fare for drive-in viewing, and when they did they often charged exorbitant fees. Hollingshead didn't do the growth of the drive-in any favors, either: he obtained a patent on his invention, charging potential operators an upfront fee plus a percentage of revenue. The

continued on page 37

Coming Soon

During their heyday in the fifties it was not at all uncommon for drive-in management to ballyhoo their coming attractions by way of little four-page leaflets/booklets. The ultimate in ephemera (i.e., meant to last but a short time; to be thrown away), not many have survived. Here, however, is a small batch - complete with definitely-meant-to-grab-your-attention-graphics - from a trio of upstate New York theatres.

34

Let's See What's Playing At The Drive-In
Part of a column of movie ads from the Bergen *(New Jersey)* Events Record, *June 9, 1950. It was not terribly difficult to tell which of the theatres was a drive-in.*

"Two Smash Hits"
From a high of almost 5,000 units in the late 1950s, the drive-in's numbers have shrunk to just over 1,000 in operation, according to National Association of Theater Owner statistics, in the summer of 1990. But, happy to say, industry experts believe the decline has leveled: that the novelty of VCRs has worn off, that the rush to gobble up suburban land for other uses has slowed, and that babyboomers - with their offspring in tow - want to relive their youth.

result was that drive-in theatres were few and very far between, with an estimated less than fifty in operation in the entire country by the time World War II - and gas rationing, which really put a crimp in the drive-in business-rolled around.

In the late forties and early fifties, however, the drive-in's fortunes changed considerably. First came the burgeoning growth of auto-related business: in the wake of post-war prosperity everyone, it seemed, had a car and everyone, it seemed, wanted to spend as much time as possible in it. Secondly, in 1949 the U.S. Supreme Court ruled that the drive-in theatre was not a patentable idea. Open air theatres could now be built by anybody who wanted to build one. And a lot of people decided they wanted to. Growth was explosive.

From a peak of close to five-thousand units in operation in 1958, the drive-in industry has shrunk. Considerably. Television, video rentals, "passion pit" reputation... all have taken their toll. Escalating real estate values on the urban fringe - prime turf for drive-ins - has also hurt considerably. Plus, there's the very nature of the drive-in: it's seasonal in much of the country; dependent upon good weather in all of it.

Still, on a warm summer night, there's nothing quite like rounding up the family and a repast...and taking in a double feature at the drive-in.

Drive-In Theatre
Route 22 near
Union, New Jersey,
July, 1947

The Tea Room

A circa 1930 photo of the Bay View Tea Room,
Route 9W, Cornwall, New York

Precursor of Today's Family Restaurant

The Tea Room

Back when Roy Rogers (real name: Leonard Slye) was still in knee pants - long before he was riding the range as a cowboy hero and long, long before the restaurants bearing his name dotted America - the tea room was all the rage. It was, in most respects, the predecessor of the family restaurant as we know it today.

Originated circa World War I, the tea room brought graciousness to roadside dinning. Often owned and operated by women, the typical tea room featured "tasteful" decor, "wholesome" atmosphere, and a larger selection of food than lunch wagons, luncheonettes, or roadside stands. But tea rooms were often pricey. And they were also quite often a bit too quaint and genteel. By the 1930s they were - in name if not in spirit - on their way to becoming a thing of the past.

Generally owned and run by ladies, the tea room typically held more appeal for them as well. Men were wont to hold them in disfavor; would often speed up if one came into view while they were behind the wheel.

Advertisement from 1934, Rome, New York

Pan Tree Tea Room
Home Cooking and Pastries
Luncheon 65c — 45c   Dinner $1.00
Special Supper 65c

Phone 1409-J
For Club Reservations, etc.   164 Washington Street

Tiffany's T Room
UPPER FRONT STREET
SPECIAL BLUE PLATE DINNER
Of Home Fried Chicken, Broilers or Chops 75c - $1.00
SPECIAL SUNDAY DINNER—$1.00-$1.25
Bridge Parties and Clubs Entertained   Phone 136-M

DARK-EYED SUSAN TEA ROOM
173 Washington Street, Second Floor
Noonday Luncheons, 65c and 45c.
Special Steak Dinner Saturday Night 1.00.
Bridge Luncheons and Afternoon Tea.
Catering to Private Parties at All Times.
For Reservations Phone 2974-W

THE
RAINBOW
TEA HOUSE

48 McKeel Avenue   Turn right at Pierson's cor.
Tarryton-on-Hudson, N. Y.

Luncheon 12 to 2   - $1.00 and $1.50
Sunday Night Supper from 6 P. M. -$1.50
For reservations Phone Tarrytown 783-W before 9 A. M.

"Bridge Luncheons and Afternoon Tea"
A page of typical tea room ads of the twenties and thirties. The grouping of three on the top were all from a 1929 Guide to Binghamton (New York). Quaintness prevailed. Not quaint, however, was the misspelling of Tarrytown in the 1930 Rainbow Tea Room advertisement.

"Let's go in and raise hell!"

"We Invite Criticism"
A splendid Click *magazine (which billed itself as "The National Picture Monthly") cartoon from 1939, in the waning years of the tea room's popularity. What makes it splendid: tea rooms were just not the sort of place where one would "raise hell."*

41

"The Most Popular Place In Town"

A wonderful pair of views of Amsterdam, New York's White Tower as it appeared in October of 1941. On his notes the photographer ventured that the Tower was "the most popular place in town." Begun in 1926, White Tower grew - at its peak in the mid-fifties - to over two-hundred thirty units, spread from Minneapolis to Boston.

You See Them Everywhere

The Ubiquitous Chain

Last in this series of roadside vignettes is the chain. However, while it's presented at the end of this loosely-chronological roadside review - due to its relatively recent rise to roadside prominence - the chain could just as accurately have been first or second in sequence. The chain goes back a long, long time. Fred Harvey saw to that.

Fred Harvey was an English immigrant who came to America in 1850 at the age of eighteen. Starting out as a $2.00-a-week dishwasher, he gradually moved up the restaurant ladder until, in 1859, he became co-proprietor of a restaurant in St. Louis. When his partner absconded with the enterprise's funds several years later, Harvey found employ as an on-board railroad mail sorting clerk, followed by a number of positions as agent for various rail lines in the Kansas/Missouri area. In all of these endeavors he was exposed to the various eating establishments with which rail travelers of the day had to contend. Fred Harvey was not impressed. He, along with a new partner, decided they could offer far better fare. And, indeed, so they did. Beginning with three units along the Kansas Pacific line in the early 1870s, Harvey Houses branched out throughout the west. By the year of his death, 1901, there were a solid forty-five Harvey units in operation across a dozen states.

It took the lunchroom, however, to really get the chain concept rolling. Ordinary, ho hum, functional; the lunchroom provided light meals quickly

Fast Food

Sometimes it seems as if "fast food" were a strictly recent phenomenon ... a concept drummed up by McDonald's, Burger King and their counterparts to coincide with America's passion for being on the go.

Not so. I am constantly amazed at how often "quick" shows up in advertisements from the twentieth century's first decades. Admittedly, their idea of "quick" and "fast" may have been different than our's, but still the message was clear: if you were in a hurry...no need to worry!

to a bustling, ever-more industrial America from the 1880s on. And while a proprietor was not likely to earn a whole heck of a lot with one outlet, he/she could begin to post some impressive figures by adding more units. The economies of scale were not lost on early lunchroom magnates. James A. Whitcomb ran with his Baltimore Dairy Lunch in the last decades of the 1800s. By the early 1920s it had grown to over one-hundred units in Baltimore and other cities. Brothers Samuel and William Childs started the operation that yet bears their name - it began as Childs Unique Dairy Lunch - in New York City in 1889, had over eighty units in full sway by 1920. In 1891, John R. Thompson, Jr. purchased the first of what grew to be over a one-hundred unit Thompson's Restaurant chain within two and a half decades. Waldorf Lunch, the brainchild of one Harry S. Kelsey, first saw the light of day in 1904 and had grown to be

"The Best of Everything is None too Good for our Patrons."

J. SILVERMAN,
Leading
Coffee and Oyster House,
12-14 East Market Street,
Wilkes-Barre, Pa.

I make a specialty of serving the best 20c meal in the City.
Quick Lunches of all kinds at all hours.

1899

Fine Food
Quick SERVICE Low PRICES

LIGHT LUNCH
A MEAL IN A MINUTE

PEDRICK'S QUICK LUNCH
Open Day and Night

48 North Main Street   Gloversville, New York

1917

The Ruggles Quick Lunch Chair
That "move 'em in and move 'em out" is not a new food service concept is most aptly demonstrated by this 1916 equity raising advertisement from H.B. Ruggles Company. Rigid and with no arm rest, the Ruggles Chair - actually more a stool - undoubtedly did the trick.

seventy-five units strong - throughout the northeast - by 1920.

The cafeteria was another type of eatery that lent itself to multi-unit operation. The Boos Brothers established a small chain of them in California starting in 1906. Bishop's was begun by Franklin Bishop in Waterloo, Iowa in 1920. In that same year, S & W was inaugurated in Charlotte, North Carolina, while Morrison's - the kingpin of all cafeteria chains today - was started in Mobile, Alabama by J.A. Morrison.

The 1920s also saw the birth of that pre-eminent American institution:

the low price/high volume hamburger stand. Appropriately enough, it started in the Heartland. It was 1921 and Wichita, Kansas entrepreneurs Walter Anderson and Edgar Waldo "Billy" Ingram felt America was ready for the advent of clean (and what connotes "clean" more than the color white?) and distinctive-looking (and what's more distinctive than a castle?) and reliable "eating houses." They were correct: from one tiny (15' by 10') cement block structure in Wichita, White Castle mushroomed to one-hundred fifteen units by 1931. Omaha, Kansas City, St. Louis, Minneapolis-St. Paul, Cincin-

nati, Louisville, Indianapolis, Detroit, Chicago, Newark, and New York City were all enjoying 5¢ hamburgers. "Buy 'em by the sack" was White Castle's slogan. And people did.

Imitators were not long in appearing on the scene. White Tower was started in Milwaukee in 1926 by father and son team of John E. (J.E.) and Thomas E. (T.E.) Saxe; the first Little Tavern was opened up in Louisville in 1927; Toddle House made its first appearance, in Houston, in 1929; etc.; etc. America was on its way to hamburger heaven.

Seven Decades Later
White Castle, the chain that gave birth to the low price/high volume hamburger stand, is still going strong at age seventy. Headquartered in Columbus, Ohio, the White Castle System, Inc. operates some 247 units in sixteen major markets, including New York City, Long Island, New Jersey and Philadelphia.

Under construction: a new McDonald's going up, Binghamton, New York, March, 1963.

Seventy-five Billion Burgers Later

Think of chains, of course, and you're most likely to think of McDonald's. The very first McDonald's, opened up by brothers Maurice ("Mac") and Richard McDonald in San Bernardino, California several years before World War II, was just your basic curb service drive-in restaurant. After the war, however, in 1948, the brothers made a bold move: having noted the success of self-service grocery shopping and self-service gas stations they decided to follow suit. They cut both service and their menu selection to a bare minimum, stressing speed and low prices. It worked. By the early fifties the brothers were serving up - in assembly-line fashion - an estimated one million hamburgers a year. Franchising - and Ray Kroc - allowed McDonald's to become the national (actually international!) giant that it is, but the basic idea of limited fare served in a jiffy remains much the same as when Mac and Richard first tried it on for size back in 1948.

Lodging, Too

Food service establishments were not, of course, the only roadside entity to witness the coming of the chain. Lodging, too, has become heavily "chained." A trip down most any strip into most any town is almost bound to yield many of the same lodging choices: Days Inn, Red Roof, Motel 6, Ramada, Howard Johnson's, Susse Chalet, Super 8, etc. etc.... and especially, of course, that granddaddy of them all, Holiday Inn. Founded in Memphis in 1952 by Kemmons Wilson (who, the story goes, had recently enjoyed the classic Bing Crosby film Holiday Inn *when he was casting about for a name for his concept of a string of uniform and reliable motor lodges), there are now over 1,600 Holiday Inns nationwide. Try going somewhere - anywhere - without finding one!*

Circa 1960 postcard

A Scrapbook of Yesterday

There was a richness to America in the 1930s and 1940s and into the 1950s. Sure, we had a Depression and a World War. Life had its perils. But we had a richness of choice. There was a host of made-right-here-in-America automobiles from which to choose. (Remember Nash and Hudson and Willys? And Kaiser? And Studebaker? Who could forget Studebaker? And how about Crosley and Packard and

Essex and ...?) There were hundreds and hundreds of different soft drink brands (and they weren't all called Coke and Pepsi). There were scores and scores of brands of locally-brewed beer and ale (and porter and bock). And, perhaps most important of all, there were real roadside choices. Mom and Pop - not corporate America - ruled the road. And it was good.

This section of **MID-ATLANTIC**

ROADSIDE DELIGHTS celebrates that goodness. That richness.

Three types of graphics have been utilized. First and foremost are post-cards. They tend to project warmth, personality, and a soft, "romantic" image. Second are period photographs. You might view them as snapshots. They tend to reproduce the best. Third are matchbook covers. They add their own style of wonderful artwork (not to

OVER ONE OF THE MANY HILLS NEAR CAZENOVIA, N. Y., ON U. S. ROUTE 20.

22

Matchbook art, 1940s

mention their often wonderful wording).

Think of the items pictured on the pages that follow as a collection from over the years. A collection lovingly gathered together and then placed in a scrapbook. As is so often the case with a scrapbook, only the barest essentials are noted. Location. Date. Wording from the address side of postcards. Not much more.

Are these places still in business? Still alive? A scrapbook doesn't tell. Sometimes, I think, things really are better when left to the imagination.

Postcard art, 1940s/1950s

One additional note: the Scrapbook is arranged alphabetically by name of roadside stop, with all three states joined together (and with eight in-color pages arranged the same way in its own separate section). I think of it as the One Big Happy Region approach.

Basher's Service Station
Route 20
Lancaster, N.Y.

1939 photograph

Four-year old Richie Basher behind the pumps at his dad's service station. For more on Basher's Service please see page 115.

Blue Diner
Paxtonia, Pa.

Circa 1950 postcard view

"Fast Service-Good Food-Reasonably Priced"

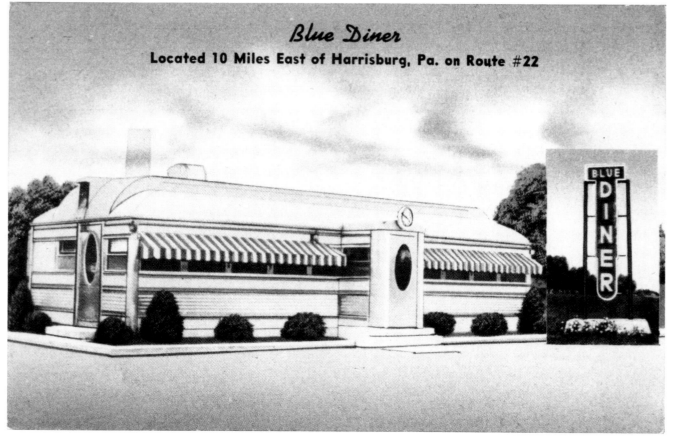

Blue Diner
Located 10 Miles East of Harrisburg, Pa. on Route #22

Brooker's Maple Shade
Main Street
Armonk, N.Y.

Circa 1925 photograph

Noted for its sign:
"Eat here - Diet Home."

Cal's Restaurant
Saegertown, Pa.

Circa 1955 matchbook cover

Centennial Diner
Atlantic City, N.J.

Circa 1955 postcard view

"The Showplace of the Playground of the World"/"Our Food and Coffee is the Talk of the Walk."

CHRISTY'S RESTAURANT — BALTIMORE PIKE — U.S. No. 1, 202 and 322   SA-H755

Christy's Restaurant
Glen Mills, Pa.

Circa 1935 postcard view

"Really a place for a mother, sister or sweetheart. Once you stop at this magnificent place it will always remain in your memory."

Cloister Diner
Route 322 — 1 block off Route 222
(At Ephrata Cloisters)
EPHRATA, PENNA.

CLOISTER

Cloister Diner
Ephrata, Pa.

Circa 1950 postcard view

Club Diner
Route 309
Quakertown, Pa.

Artwork from inside cover, circa 1955 matchbook

Good FOOD

Low PRICES
Quick SERVICE

FRIED COUNTRY HAM PLATTERS
Phone 459

The Coffee Pot
New Bedford, Pa.

September, 1943 photograph

The photographer's caption notes The Coffee Pot as "an eating place near the Greyhound bus stop."

Colonial Diner
Stroudsburg, Pa.

June, 1947 photograph

Cramer's Cabins
Fenelton, Pa.

Circa 1950 postcard view

"Pennsylvania's Finest"/
"Every Modern Con-
venience. Hot and Cold
Water, Steam and Gas
Heat, Shower Baths in
Each Cabin, Beautyrest
Mattresses, Hardwood
Floors, Electric Lights."

Cramer's
CABINS

14 DELUXE UNITS
7 Miles East of Butler, Pa., on U. S. Route 422

Crew Levick Service Station
1635 Union Boulevard
Allentown, Pa.

September, 1929 photograph

One of three Crew Levick Cities
Service stations in operation in
Allentown at the time.

Daddy Bill's, The Igloo
Saw Mill River Road
Ardsley, N.Y.

Circa 1947 photograph

Inspired by a building he had seen at the 1939
World's Fair, Edward Aim constructed The Igloo
that same year. From it he (and later Daddy Bill
Brinkerhoff) sold apple cider, hot dogs, and, not
surprisingly, frozen custard.

Danny's Drive-In Restaurant
Schenectady, N.Y.

Circa 1950 matchbook cover

"Curb Service...On Roller Skates"

Dave Baird Texaco
Camp Road
Hamburg, N.Y.

1940 photograph

Deer Trail
Gaines, Pa.

Circa 1930 postcard view

DEER TRAIL, 18 MILES WEST OF WELLSBORO, PA., ON ROOSEVELT HIGHWAY.

Dave's Dream

RESTAURANT & BAR-B-QUE
Located 4 Miles from Harrisburg, Pa.
On the Hershey By-pass Route #422

Dave's Dream
Harrisburg, Pa.

Circa 1950 postcard view

Ebby's Diner
Lancaster, Pa.

February, 1942 photograph

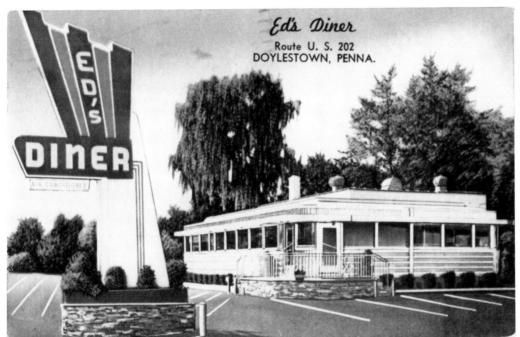

Ed's Diner
Doylestown, Pa.

Circa 1950 postcard view

"We Serve The Best, At Its Best"

Elm & Maiden Lane Gas & Oil
(a.k.a. Hopkin's Parking Station)
Penn Yan, N.Y.

Circa 1940 photograph

4th St. Diner
Syracuse vicinity, N.Y.

October, 1941 photograph

Frank's Filling Station
Bushwick Avenue and Pellington Place
Brooklyn, N.Y.

September 18, 1934 photograph

Garfield Diner
Garfield Square
Pottsville, Pa.

October, 1960 photograph

Yes, that's JFK - and a few other people, too - congregating outside the diner. The occasion: a political rally.

Gateway Diner
Phillipsburg, N.J.

Circa 1950 matchbook cover

Gearhart's Dairy Lunch
Sunbury, Pa.

Circa 1955 matchbook cover

Glen Motor Court
Route 14
Watkins Glen, N.Y.

Circa 1950 postcard view

"Deluxe Motel and Cabins, 28 units, private toilets and showers with plenty of hot water, overlooking beautiful Seneca Lake, one of the finest scenic views in America."

Grand View - Ship Hotel on U. S. 30, the only Steamboat in the Mountains in U. S.

GRAND VIEW POINT HOTEL

SEE 3 STATES and 7 COUNTIES

17 Miles West of Bedford, Pa., 80 Miles East of Pittsburgh, Pa.

3A-H777

Grand View Point Hotel and Restaurant
Central City, Pa.

Circa 1940s' postcard views

The brainchild of a man who loved the sea, "Captain" Herbert Paulson, the Grand View Point opened on Memorial Day, 1932. An estimated 500,000 visitors stopped by during the course of the day to help "launch" it.

Main Dining Room, S. S. Grand View Point Hotel on Lincoln Highway, 17 Miles West of Bedford, Pa.

8A-H2769

63 Mile View from Grand View Point Ship Hotel on Lincoln Highway

PA.   MD.   W. VA.

GRAND VIEW POINT HOTEL   SEE 3 STATES and 7 COUNTIES

17 Miles West of Bedford, Pa., Looking into 3 States and 7 Counties

4A-H1905

Green Acres
Wexford, Pa.

Circa 1955 matchbook cover

Gus' Michigan Red Hots
Route 9 and Cumberland
Head Corners
Plattsburgh, N.Y.

1951 photograph

That's proud proprietor Gus Neforos in front.

BLACK CAT — ABSECON, NEW JERSEY

BA-H1006

Black Cat
Absecon, New Jersey

Circa 1950 postcard view

"7 miles from Atlantic City;
50 from Philadelphia;
108 from New York"

Nicholson Rd. & Black Horse Pk.
W. Collingswood Heights, New Jersey
Phone: GLoucester 6-1242

ALWAYS
OPEN

AIR
CONDITIONED

Black Horse Diner
West Collingswood Heights,
New Jersey

Circa 1955 postcard view

"When in this vicinity, Whatever
the hour, Stop and Visit us.
Good food is Well Served in
a Clean Air-conditioned
Atmosphere. Be it a Sandwich
or a Full Course Meal we will
do our utmost to make your
visit a pleasant one."

Blue Bird Restaurant, Chambersburg, Pa.

**Blue Bird Restaurant
Chambersburg, Pa.**

Circa 1955 postcard view

Fernwood DINER EAST LANSDOWNE, PA.

**Fernwood Diner
East Lansdowne, Pa.**

Circa 1950 postcard view

"Hoping You Have Enjoyed
Your Dinner With Us. We
Thank You For Your Patronage.
Ernest Schilling & His Employees"

Golden Arrow Diner
Route 1
Langhorne, Pa.

Circa 1948 postcard view

"Look For The 'Golden Arrow' On The Lincoln Highway"

Johnson's Restaurant
Bradford, Pa.

Circa 1955 matchbook cover

Kendall Tourist Camp
Silver Creek, N.Y.

Circa 1950 postcard view

"Consisting of 49 Furnished Cottages, free Tourist Kitchen and large Service Station: ideally located in the Heart of one of America's Garden Spots."

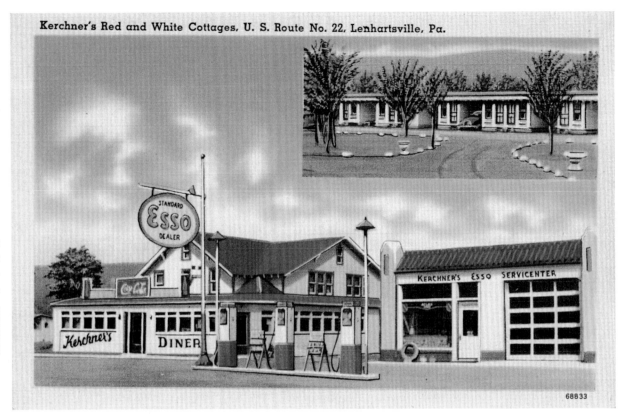

Kerchner's Red and White Cottages, U. S. Route No. 22, Lenhartsville, Pa.

68833

Kerchner's Red and White Cottages, Diner, and Esso Servicenter Lenhartsville, Pa.

Circa 1945 postcard view

"We have 16 Cottages and Rooms with Simmons Beds, Innerspring Mattresses, Automatic Hot Water Heat, Private Bath Rooms, and Garages."

SINGLE AND DOUBLE CABINS

8A-H2486

The Marilorn Barbeque and Tourist Home Waverly, N.Y.

THE MARILORN BARBECUE AND TOURIST HOME — ROUTE No. 17 — WAVERLY, N. Y.

New Towers Hotel and Diner
West Nanticoke, Pa.

Circa 1955 postcard view

"All Conveniences for the traveling public including meals and modern rooms, with hot and cold water in each room."

Niagara Falls Boulevard Motor Hotel, Tonawanda, N.Y.

Circa 1955 postcard view

"Special Rates to Clergymen, Honeymooners and Traveling Salesmen."

PATRICK'S DINER
Highland New York

Patrick's Diner
Route 9W
Highland, N.Y.

Circa 1950 postcard view

"The Most Modern Diner in Ulster County. Opened Jan. 3, 1946. Tony Patrick & Sons, Prop."

Rhinebeck Diner
Rhinebeck, N.Y.

Circa 1945 postcard view

"Largest and most modern diner in State, built at a cost of $65,000. Opened May 7, 1938. Serving best food with cleanliness our Motto. T. Djinis, Prop."

RHINEBECK DINER — ROUTE U.S. 9 — RHINEBECK, N.Y.   OB-H1583

Rose Haven Courts
Gloucester City, N.J.

Circa 1955 postcard view

"South Jersey's Finest Tourist Court: Moderate Rates and True Hospitality."

Schlenker Service Station, Restaurant and Cabins Hamburg, Pa.

Circa 1950 postcard view

"24 Hour Service/Tourists Accommodated/Sales and Service for Ford-Mercury and Lincoln-Zephyr Cars/We specialize in Home Cooking."

Texaco Grille
Woodworth's Restaurant
Geneva, N.Y.

Circa 1955 postcard view

Texaco Grille: "Fifteen
years of 24 hour Diner
Service"
Woodworth's: "A Bite or
a Banquet."

Shaffer's Snack Bar
Sayre, Pa.

Circa 1955 match-
book cover

Trent Diner
Route 1, north
Trenton, N.J.

Circa 1955 postcard view

"The most beautiful Diner
in the world"

Ham That Am Restaurant
Chittenango, N.Y.

Circa 1955 postcard view

The Original HAM THAT AM HAM RESTAURANT

15 MILES EAST OF SYRACUSE ON ROUTE 5, CHITTENANGO, N.Y.

E-5956

Howard Johnson's Restaurant
Route 46
Essex County, N.J.

July, 1947 photograph

Jack's Lunch
North Street
Middletown, N.Y.

Circa 1916 photograph

"Jack" was John M. "Jack" Gaynor (that's he on the front left), a bit of an eatery entrepreneur around Middletown from 1908 through at least the 1930s. He, at one time or another, owned a diner, a restaurant, a hotel, and, of course, the spiffy-looking lunch wagon pictured here.

Jim & Bill's Modern Mari-May Diner
Rosemont, Pa.

Circa 1955 postcard view

"Completely Air-Conditioned - Open 24 Hrs. - Delicious Food - Serving Meals At All Times"

Jo-Em-Ma-Do Court
Harrisburg, Pa.

Circa 1955 postcard view

It was family all the way here:
the motel's name stands for
Joanne, Emmett, Martha, and Donald...
the Ulrich family, proprietors.

Keystone Restaurant
Corry, Pa.

Circa 1955 matchbook cover

Lawrence Tourist Cabins
Chester, N.Y.

Circa 1950 postcard view

"25 deluxe heated cabins. Hot showers and
individual toilets, kitchenette, inner-spring
mattresses."

Lemoyne Diner
Route 111
Lemoyne, Pa.

Circa 1955 postcard view

"Across the Scenic
Susquehanna River from
Harrisburg, the State Capital."

Miami Motel and Drive-In Restaurant
Albany Avenue Boulevard/Route 40
West Atlantic City, N.J.

Circa 1950 postcard view

"Wall to Wall Carpeting, Colored
ceramic tiled Baths, Telephones,
Air Conditioning, TV Lobby,
Swimming Pool. 3 Minutes ride
from Boardwalk."

Minnich's Gulf
West High and North Pitt Streets
Carlisle, Pa.

Circa 1950 photograph

Mobil Gasoline Station
10th Street (between
6th and 7th Avenues)
Beaver Falls, Pa.

April, 1945 photograph

Left to right that's
Jack Karcher, Bill Shields,
and Wilford Milnes.

OLD HIGHTS RESTAURANT

103 MAIN ST., HIGHTSTOWN, N. J.

OC-H1332

Old Hights Restaurant
Hightstown, N.J.

Circa 1950 postcard view

"A Cuisine of Excellence -
Delightful Atmosphere -
Courteous Service."

Penn State Flyer Diner
Allentown, Pa.

Billboard photograph, May, 1945

Parkway Diner
Union, N.J.

Circa 1955
matchbook
cover

Phil & Ernie's Service Station
Coney Island Avenue
Brooklyn, N.Y.

June, 1940 photographs

The Pig Stand

A MEAL AT YOUR WHEEL

SERVING
CENTRAL N. Y.
FOR OVER
25 YEARS

Pig Sandwich

TRADE MARK
REGISTERED
DEWITT, N. Y.

WHERE
GOOD FOOD
TASTES
BETTER

The Pig Stand
Route 5
DeWitt, N.Y.

July, 1955 photographs, plus menu heading

Famed for its pork, beef, and turkey barbeque, the Pig Stand was open seven days a week, from 11:00 AM until 3:00 AM; heralded itself as "America's Motor Lunch."

Red Bridge Tourist Court
Route 11, north
Chambersburg, Pa.

Circa 1945 postcard view

Reichard & Sandike Sunoco
Unadilla, N.Y.

Circa 1950 double postcard

Spot Oil Company Richfield Station
Route 11, between Cortland and Homer, N.Y.

Circa 1935 photograph

The sign that hangs out front reads "Richfield - The Gasoline of Power."

Rice's Diner
West State Street
Ithaca, N.Y.

Circa 1945 photograph

Riverside Diner
144 South Main Street/Route 11
Homer, N.Y.

October, 1945 photograph

"This diner depends on truckers for its trade,"
noted the photographer.

S.D.S. Grill
Binghamton, N.Y.

Circa 1942 matchbook cover, showing both outside and inside art and wording.

Sheeler's Garage
616 East Gay Street
West Chester, Pa.

May, 1947 photograph

Sky-Way Drive-In Theatre
5314 West Lake Road
Millcreek Township, Pa.

Circa 1950 photograph

Sterling Diners of Rochester, N.Y.
Rochester, N.Y.

Circa 1945 matchbook cover

Sunset Diner
Route 22
Plainfield vicinity, N.J.

Billboard photograph, 1945

Three Gables Service Station and Restaurant
Camp Hill, Pa.

Circa 1950 postcard view

"Featuring Hospitality, Service and Good Food."

Twin Grill
Scranton, Pa.

Circa 1950 matchbook cover and inside cover

Vivi Gas Stations
Rego Park and Long
Island City (Queens), N.Y.

Circa 1940 matchbook cover

Walp's Restaurant and Guest House
Allentown, Pa.

Circa 1950 postcard view

"One of the best places to eat between New York
and Pittsburgh."

Walt's
Route 46
Essex County, N.J.

July, 1947 photograph

WATER GAP LUNCH — WHERE YOU SEE THE SUSQUEHANNA

NORTH OF DAUPHIN, PA.

OC-H694

Water Gap Lunch
Route 22
Dauphin, Pa.

Circa 1950 postcard view

"Recommended by Truckers and Tourists alike."

Wampsville Dairy Bar
Wampsville, N.Y.

Circa 1955 matchbook cover

Westchester Diner
Saw Mill River Road
Ardsley, N.Y.

Circa 1933 photograph

The Westchester Diner arrived in Ardsley in 1923. Longtime proprietors were Angelo and Anna DeMilo. That's Anna and Junior (and tricycle) posing outside the entrance.

White Tower
219-44 Hillside Avenue
Queens Village, N.Y.

Circa 1940 photograph

White Tower
147-01 Liberty Avenue
Jamaica, N.Y.

Circa 1936 photograph

Present-day Delights

Nostalgia's nice. There's nothing quite like the old-time photo and postcard views that grace the *Scrapbook Of Yesterday* section of *MID-ATLANTIC ROADSIDE DELIGHTS*. But there's nothing wrong with the present, either. Amidst the seemingly endless barrage of all-from-the-same-mold McDonald's, Arby's, Burger Kings, Taco Bells, Pizza Huts, Holiday Inns, etc., etc., etc. there are some individualistic and wonderful roadside stops out there.

The places included over the next sixty-six pages are my favorites, discovered via a lot of wandering and a lot of conversations with a lot of people. They're not meant to constitute a complete list of all of the region's delights. They are certainly, however, a plentitude of the very best roadside still up and operating. They're, for the most part, places that made me want to say "Wow;" places that I found visually attractive. (Note: no attempt, it should be made clear, has been made to review culinary artistry: although I did eat in many of the establishments listed and found them to be universally very good.). They're also places that are not located within the city limits of the region's "big five": New York City, Philadelphia, Pittsburgh, Buffalo, or Newark. There's "roadside" and there's "streetside"...and I decided, in this section at least, to concentrate on roadside.

So come on along: let's go to Shamokin, Pennsylvania where it's still 1918 at the Coney Island Lunch; to Heid's in Liverpool, New York where you're likely to want to bring your hula hoop and blue suede shoes; to the Circle Drive-In Theatre in Dickson City, Pennsylvania where the marquee is so dazzling you may just want to admire *it* all night. There're marvelous diners, curb service drive-ins, cabin courts, big places and little places, wonderful places. As the saying goes, there's something for everybody.

Points of Selection/Points of View

1 - The places selected are *among* the region's best...not necessarily *all of* the best. I'm certain that I've overlooked some wonderful spots. But that doesn't mean that you have to. Support your local diner and mom and pop hot dog, hamburger and/or ice cream stand. If there's a drive-in theatre near you, patronize it. Without business, these places will fail...and we could find ourselves with one big Mc/Bur/Arb/KFC/Tac/PizHut/Roy stand/restaurant. Ugh.

2 - There is an ever-increasing herd of large and ornate diner-restaurants throughout the region. You know the ones I mean: they're usually dressed up in an abundance of fake stone, promise "all baking done on premises," and have names like Conquistador or La Mirage. None of these have been included.

3 - Places that have been "done over" or modernized have been largely excluded. To modernize, sad to say, is generally to uglify.

4 - I've tried to limit selections to places that have remained what they started out to be: diners that began as diners and still are; gas stations that yet serve as gas stations, etc.

5 - There are eight pages (121 to 128) of places photographed in color in the middle of the section. Roadside can be very, very colorful!

You'll be smiling, too, when you patronize your local diner or drive-in or other roadside neighbor. They do it all for you.

New Jersey

Camaraderie abounded in many of the diners and other establishments that I visited in my travels. It seemed to especially abound at the **WHITE CRYSTAL**, 20 Center Avenue, **ATLANTIC HIGHLANDS** (7 miles NE of Red Bank). Everybody appeared to know everybody, conversation and bantering flowed, warmth was in the air. No one is more appreciative of it all than White Crystal proprietor Tony Natale, who has worked in the diner business since he was ten years old. As Tony philosophized, in explaining what so intrigues him about diners, is that you get to meet people from all walks of life: "You can have a lawyer next to a postal worker next to a doctor and everyone will talk to each other. It's a real form of open discussion."

The White Crystal is a 1960 Kullman (Kullman Dining Car Company, Harrison, New Jersey) with fifteen stools spread over two counters. Inside it's heavy on baby blue; outside it's all stainless and, of course, white. Tony's been there since the beginning, working for his dad, Joe, from 1960 until 1973. In that year, Joe passed

Tony and his staff: that's his mother, Molly Natale, on the left; Maryann Cambeis on the right.

away and Tony's owned and operated the diner since. (Incidentally, Joe Natale had owned a diner on Route 36 in Middletown Township for many years before he set up the White Crystal. It was to have been called Natale's Diner, but the signmaker made a mistake and it came out "Natalie's Diner" instead. Joe told the signmaker, "You take $75 off and I'll keep it." The signmaker did. And so did Joe. Such, sometimes at least, is how names are come by.).

I don't really know why, but I found myself "underwhelmed" with the dark red and gold exterior of *ANGIE'S BRIDGETON GRILL*, 1½ East Broad Street, **BRIDGETON**. The interior of this Silk City (Paterson Vehicle

Company, Paterson, New Jersey), though, is another story. There's snappy-looking blue and gray floor and wall tiling, a preponderance of wood trim, sliding wooden windows (a la a train), and three ceiling fans that certainly look old enough to be original. Very enticing.

BURLINGTON TOWNSHIP: please see page 102.

Were there a Mid-Atlantic Roadside Landscape Award it would almost certainly go to *HOT DOG JOHNNY'S*, Route 46, **BUTTZVILLE** (8 miles NW of Washington). The grounds are that beautiful: shrubs, flowers, lawn areas, hanging plants, swings, picnic tables... all on the banks of the Pequest River.

Lovely as the grounds are, however, people come to Hot Dog Johnny's for its hot dogs, served out of the good-looking round green concrete structure that John Kovalsky built in 1947. Although somewhat overshadowed by several eating-room wings that have been added on through the years, the 1947 building is still the focal point. It, though, is actually Johnny's number two. Number one, a small shed of a structure, was located about a half mile or so further east, and was in use in 1944 and 1945.

Hot Dog Johnny's is today run by John's daughter and son-in-law, Pat and George Fotopoulous. It opens at 8:30 AM ("You'd be surprised how many people eat hot dogs for breakfast," notes Pat.) three-hundred sixty-two days of the year, closing only on Thanksgiving, Christmas, and New Year's. Hot dogs (the special comes with mustard, onion, and a hearty slice of fresh pickle!), French fries, birch beer, buttermilk, and soda are the order of the day.

So, of course, is the landscaping.

Sign on Route 46 announcing Hot Dog Johnny's.

Pat and employees Michael Alampi, left, and Frank Dragotta, right. Pat started in at age eight, born into a real success story: her dad, then twenty-five, got the idea of going into hot dogs while shooting a game of pool in neighboring Belvidere in 1943. After looking around the area, he fixed upon a service station location near the intersection of Routes 46 and 31, persuading the station's owner to allow him to set up business on the station's sidelines. Opening on Palm Sunday, 1944, he grossed $80.00 for the day and told his wife, Louise, "If we stick with this we'll have the world where we want it." Stick with it he did!

97

It's somewhat weathered now, but the eight-foot tall neon sign that is meant to beckon passersby to the *TWIN KISS DRIVE-IN*, South Delsea Drive/ Route 47, **CLAYTON** (5 miles SE of Glassboro) is yet worthy of note. The words "Soft" and "Ice Cream" plus the sign's outline are in red neon, while "Twin Kiss" is in white, and an arrow (pointing the way to the stand) is in baby blue. Proprietor Mary Kasper dates the sign to the late 1950s.

In **ELMWOOD PARK** (2 miles E of Paterson) in search of an old gas station - which turned out to have been demolished - I was instead rewarded with a nice find in the *RIVER VIEW EAST*, 455 River Drive, a largish circa 1950 white with red trim building. Owned and operated by partners Michael Tsistrakis and Thomas DeCicco, the River View projects an appearance that is semi-streamlined, punctuated by "River View East"

spelled out in large red neon letters. The specialty: a hot Texas Weiner with the works... mustard, onions, and home-made chili sauce.

It's a place one could fairly easily pass by, but something struck my fancy about the circa 1950 KUSTARD KORNER, Route 50 and Fairmont Avenue, EGG HARBOR CITY. Perhaps it's the all-whiteness of it. Perhaps it's the dramatic wooden "Kustard Korner" sign - complete with five-foot cone - that's atop the roof. Whatever it is, I found myself admiring the Kustard Korner more than the many other ice cream stands I ran across in the Garden State.

HOENES SERVICE, White Horse Pike/Route 30 and Cologne Street, COLOGNE (4 miles SE of Egg Harbor City), is an exceedingly well-maintained Tudor-influenced white stucco and brick building that probably dates from the late thirties, although the business goes back to October of 1930 when George Hoenes, Sr. opened a pint-sized Cities Service station on

the site. Not only is the station, now owned and operated by George Hoenes, Jr., lovely to look at, it sits amid what could almost be called landscaped grounds. There are even potted plants between the pumps! Look inside and you'll be pleased, too: there are several nice old period photos - of the station in its younger days - up on the wall for all to admire.

Tony Iliadis at the grill. To see his Freehold Grill, FREEHOLD, please turn to page 121.

Red and white stripes are the order of the day at *ANGELO'S DINER*, 16 North Main Street, **GLASSBORO**. A 1941 Kullman (Kullman Dining Car Company, Harrison, New Jersey), Angelo's otherwise stainless exterior is graced with red and white striped awnings, while the diner itself is set into a circa 1910 two-story building that is also bedecked with red and white striped awnings. A nice oval "Angelo's Diner" neon corner sign rounds out a real homey spot. Originally owned and operated by Angelo and Helen Tubertini, the diner remained in the family when Angelo passed away in 1980: today's owner/operators are Mary Ann (Angelo and Helen's daughter) and Joe Justice. The red and white was Joe's idea. "It just fit," he explained. I agree.

Joe and Mary Ann Justice behind the counter at Angelo's.

The White Manna: as the sign says, the specialty is hamburgers. The tiny eat-'em-by-the-half-dozen size. And that's just what the storied diner's patrons do.

Many a diner has lead more than one life. Such is certainly the case with the **WHITE MANNA**, 358 River Street, **HACKENSACK**. Life number one was as a showcase: it was constructed by the Jerry O'Mahony diner manufacturing company in 1937 to serve as a prototype for the diner of the future at the 1939/1940 New York World's Fair. Serve as prototype it did: introducing millions to the wonders of stainless steel, glass block, porcelain counters and fluorescent lighting.

Life number two is Hackensack all the way. It arrived in 1947 and its initial location was about fifty feet south of where it is now. In 1968 the diner was moved to its present site. It almost appears as if the move could've been made by a six-pack of guys from a body-building course: the White

Manna is that small. It's but sixteen feet wide, has about eight-hundred square feet. Seating capacity is twenty stools, spread over three counter areas. The major counter holds twelve of the twenty. U-shaped, it leads to a very definite feeling of togetherness. The Fenway Park of diners.

What the White Manna lacks in size, however, it more than makes up in charm. A fairly conservative - but lovely - white and red on the outside, the interior pulls out all the stops with beautiful black and orange wall tiles

and a bevy of glass block.

Brothers Ronnie and Ofer Cohen bought the Manna from longtime owner John Aldridge in 1985. They've been smart enough to change very little. They know a good thing when they see it!

"The last of the area's old pot-bellied stations" is how one of the assemblage at *LITTLE MIKE'S*, South Broad Street/Route 206 and New Cedar Lane, **HAMILTON TOWNSHIP**,

Ronnie Cohen, left, and Ron Klementowski, right, working the grill the day I was there. As Ron K. joked, "You have to be named Ron to work here."

put it the day I was there. I suspect he's right: the building, located about three-hundred yards from the Trenton line, goes back to at least the early thirties. It's an attractive red, white and blue, has a Spanish tile roof and a two-columned portico. Most noteworthy of all, however, is that it's an all steel structure. You just don't find many of those still up and operating.

HARRISON *and Max's Grill: please see page 122.*

It has seen somewhat better days, but there's still a lot of good looks left in PAL'S DINER, Route 17, MAHWAY. Both Dick Morgan, who's been the grillman at Pal's since its origins circa 1955, and Guinell McMillian, who served as part maitre'd/ part bouncer from 1965 until 1972, will tell you about the lines there used to be just to get in. Pal's was the hot spot of the area. Laughed Guinell, "If you didn't get lucky in a bar you'd try your chances here. The place used to really jump Friday and Saturday nights and on Sunday afternoon. What a crowd!"

Well, the crowds have gone. But Pal's

lavish pink neon roof sign is still worth a visit. Ask Dick to tell you about how the diner got its name. (It seems two guys, one named John and one named Bill, had been pals in the service during World War II. When they got out, in 1945-46, they took over an old Silk City diner one hundred or so yards down Route 17...and named it, logically enough, Pal's. John bought Bill out in a year, but the name stuck. And when John - whose last name was Dezury - purchased a brand new model from the Manno Dining Car Company of Belleville, New Jersey, in or around 1955 and set it up at its present site, he continued on with the same name. Once a Pal's, always a Pal's.).

There used to be three. Then there were two. Now there is one. THE BAY AVENUE DINER is the last of MANA-HAWKIN's three diners. No one is more aware of this fact than proprietors Perry and Stella Zizos: their menu, at least somewhat wistfully, proclaims that they are "The Last of Manahawkin's Diner-Saurs!" Located at 32 East Bay Avenue, just off Route 9, the Zizos' diner features an interior of red, pink and, of course, lots of stainless. The exterior is yellow, which I like. But what I like most is the Bay Avenue's wraparound windows. They project a rather sleek look on the outside; make for a bright and cheery atmosphere on the inside.

I like the color orange. I like root beer. And I like carhops. So it's no wonder that I like the bright orange *STEWART'S ROOT BEER STANDS*, featuring curb service, that enhance the New Jersey roadscape.

Begun by a teacher named Frank Stewart - as a means to make some extra money over the summer - the first Stewart's opened in Mansfield, Ohio in 1924. Only root beer and popcorn, served by carhops, were offered. Today there are fifty-one Stewart's in operation across Kentucky, Ohio, West Virginia, Pennsylvania and, especially, New Jersey. Thirty-one of the fifty-one are in the Garden State. Headquarters are also in New Jersey, in Clementon.

The Stewart's of the 1990s offers a full drive-in restaurant menu. Burgers, cheese steaks, hot dogs, chicken baskets. The full gamut. But the root beer hasn't changed. Nor has the carhop service.

The Stewart's that I found in my travels were universally handsome. A prime example is the one on Route 130 in __BURLINGTON TOWNSHIP__*. Built circa 1940, it's twenty feet square, bright orange (that's painted anew each and every year), with jet black "Root Beer" lettering. Open air, it's surrounded on all four sides by parking places for carhop service.*

Carhops: Stewart's likes them. And they like Stewart's. Rachael Grayson, who works at the Stewart's on Route 9 in TUCKERTON, began in the kitchen but switched to carhopping. She likes it because "It's fun. You get to see people you know. And you get to meet new people." Carol Navarro, a five-year veteran at the Stewart's at 584 South Delsea/Route 47, VINELAND, was more explicit: "It's fun. It's got a lot of style. It's fast. It's simple. And you make a lot of money."

Rachael Grayson, Tuckerton:
"You get to meet new people."

Carol Navarro, Vineland:
"It's got a lot of style."

Set admist the hustle/bustle of modern-day Route 4 is a tiny (seventeen feet wide by thirteen feet deep) gas station that's a throw-back to a gentler, slower time. Located at 138 West Route 4 in PARAMUS, the A.M.C. SUNOCO was probably built in the early 1930s. It was definitely built to appeal...and it does, with its own little chimney, gabled entranceway, and fresh-ly painted colors of tan, yellow, and blue. Look for it right after Chan's Wakiki Restaurant and just before the Route 17 turnoff. But look for it carefully: it's easy to miss.

A landmark. That's perhaps the best way to describe *JIM'S DOGGIE STAND*, on the scene in **PHILLIPS-BURG** since 1910. Now located at 5 Union Square (at the approach to the Easton-Phillipsburg Free Bridge), the Doggie Stand's first thirty years were spent on the opposite side of Union Square. In 1940, the business was moved to the same side as now, but closer to the river (the Delaware). That

proved a problem when, in 1966, an errant truck plowed into the stand and pushed it not just closer to the river, but - splash - into it.

There's no keeping a good hot dog stand down, though: the Doggie Stand set up again, this time on the ground floor of a quite substantial circa 1920 three-story building. That's where it is now - a marvel in its own right - sporting white pillars, old-time "The

Famous Original Frankfurter" green lettering, "Jim's Doggie Stand" in red neon, and sixty - count 'em! - yellow light bulbs.

Jim's Doggie Stand, which sells only hot dogs, soda, milk, and chips, is open every day except Tuesday, and is the place to go ("Everybody knows Jimmie's," as the staff phrased it the evening I was there) for a dog or a dozen in the Easton/Phillipsburg area.

The "Jim" of Jim's Doggie Stand was James Makris, who started in the lunch business with a hand cart in Centre Square in Easton in 1908 before moving across the river to Phillipsburg in 1910. He passed away in November of 1983 at the rather grand old age of ninety-seven.

Tim DeFilippis behind the counter and admist the pennants.

not in the sense - thank goodness - of a forty-foot television screen, but in the sense of its motif and in fostering sports discussion. Original from its beginnings (the Time Out is a 1945 Silk City) are the diner's lovely aqua, yellow and black wall tiling, and the catchy-looking ceiling vents. New with Tim are black and white striped (as with a referee's shirt) curtains, a towering "Time Out Diner" sign out front, and, back in the interior, pennants, pennants every-where: fifty-two of them when I was there, representing just about every baseball, football, and hockey team imaginable. And should the Eagles or the Phillies - Tim's a stalwart Phila-delphia fan - take home another crown, you may be sure there'll be at least another fifty-two unfurled and up and about!

TUCKERTON: *please see page 103.*

VINELAND: *please see page 103.*

There are sports bars... so why not a sports diner? Such was the reasoning of then 28-year old Tim DeFilippis in early 1989. A veteran of the food and beverage industry, an avid sports fan, and anxious to do something all his own, Tim acted upon his reasoning in September of 1989. He purchased the former Rosie's Diner, 2050 Route 50, **TUCKAHOE** (10 miles W of Ocean City), spent several months toning it up, and then, in January of 1990, re-opened as the *TIME OUT DINER*.

Here's your chance to own a piece of roadside filling station history. As of September, 1990, the POHATCONG SERVICE STATION, Route 31, WASHINGTON, was on the market. The central - and older - building is a circa 1930 22' x 17' stucco structure (adjoining is a newer two-bay garage). With a little love and attention, it could be adorable.

New York

The *KAYUTA DRIVE-IN*, Route 12, **ALDER CREEK** (11 miles SE of Boonville), is a blend of new and newer. But you'd be hard-pressed to guess it. And it carries on a tradition that goes back to the 1920s. As proprietor Jim Minosh explains it: there's been some sort of a roadside stop on the site for over three-quarters of a century. Today's stop - the Kayuta - presents a large 1980s' structure added onto a smallish white-with-red-roof building that's a fooler. It appears to be 1930s (Is it the aluminum roof that looks remarkably like Spanish tile? Or is it the neat large script "Kayuta" lettering?), but it's actually 1970s. Whatever, it's the Kayuta, and it's definitely appealing.

Great circa 1950 neon that heralds the BALDWINSVILLE DINER, BALDWIN-SVILLE (14 miles NW of Syracuse). With a background of yellow, black, orange and green, and with "B-ville Diner" spelled out in bright red neon, this truly is a sign that stands out in the crowd.

When an old time - 1946 - diner is named the Yankee Clipper, you just assume that someone was an ardent Joltin' Joe DiMaggio fan. But no, the *YANKEE CLIPPER DINER*, 397 Main Street, **BEACON**, was named in honor of the famous Pan Am Yankee Clipper. In fact, original owner James Patignes prided himself on his airplane motif cups, saucers and plates. The diner presents an exterior of white, blue, and stainless with pronounced wraparound windows. Most noticeable is the somewhat faded, but still grand, large blue "Yankee Clipper" (with the letters spelled out in red neon) sign that dominates the roofline. The interior has been completely remodeled.

Timmy Anagnostos and his sixteen-year old son, Spiro. Spiro's feelings about diner life: "It's alright."

"I believe I'm the only one around who hasn't modernized," Timmy Anagnostos reflected as he worked the grill the Sunday morning I stopped in at his ***BLUE POINT DINER***, 145 Montauk Highway/Suffolk County Route 85, **BLUE POINT** (1 mile SW of Patchogue). Judging from what else I ran across on the South Shore, I expect Timmy's correct. His diner - a 1940s' Mountain View - came as a most welcome relief. It's a crisp and attractive blue and stainless on the outside; projects a warmth and graciousness on the inside. That's largely Timmy's doing. As affable a dinerman as I've met, he's been in the food service business since his arrival in America in 1959 at age fourteen. When he had the chance to buy the Blue Point in 1986 he jumped at it. He hasn't regretted it since. (And, one suspects, the Blue Point's customers haven't either.).

BOLTON LANDING: please see page 123.

Good old gas stations sometimes come in twos. Such was certainly the case in **BUCHANAN** (1 mile SW of Peekskill). My first find was the ***ROTARY GAS STATION***, 176 Albany Post Road/Route 9A. The Rotary is almost a gas station museum. In 1927, Claire and her late husband Willard Stoddard bought the two-story house that yet serves as her home, added two rows of pumps and a large overhang, and opened up for business selling Rotary gas and kerosene. Well, Rotary is long out of operation (the station now sells Citgo), but the overhang and the pumps - the *original* pumps - are still going strong...as is Claire, who's a spry seventy-six and

The original 1927 Wayne "Honest Measure" gas pumps are yet going strong at the Rotary Gas Station in Buchanan.

who still does the pumping.

Up the hill from the Rotary, still on 9A and still in Buchanan, is another gas station, and a rather legendary one at that. It's the ***GALLON MEASURE SERVICE***, 106 Albany Post Road. What makes it legendary is the fact that

JOE HUBERTUS' MOBIL SERVICE, corner of West Main and Green Streets, **CANISTEO**, is a classic mid-1950s' box design station that is so spic and span you could safely, I suspect, eat off its floors and walls. Hubertus' is also lovely to look at, with a facade of gleaming red, white, and blue porcelainized metal highlighted by a bright red flying red horse.

the station's office is built in the shape of a gallon measure beaker. It's quite a sight: a round fourteen-foot-in-diameter-by-eighteen-foot-high white stucco building, complete with pour spout and overhanging lid. A real traffic stopper! Built circa 1926 by Ray

Gallagher, the Gallon Measure has been owned and operated - and cared for - by Richard Fay and Rom Cesnavicius since 1974. Richard, especially, is a roadside architecture devotee.

Richard Fay and Ron Cesnavicius stand - proudly - in front of their Gallon Measure.

Tucked away in the corner of the parking lot for DAR'S KITCHEN, Lake Street/Route 49, CLEVELAND (25 miles W of Rome), is this splendid example of 1940s' pop art advertising. Although the sign is a throwback to when the restaurant was called CD's, the folks at Dar's have, gloriously, left it in place. Ah, but do they still serve "America's Best Hamburger?" Only Wimpy knows for sure.

Perhaps the lovliest of Long Island's diners is the **CUTCHOGUE DINER**, Main Street/Route 25, **CUTCHOGUE** (15 miles E of Riverhead). Its exterior sparkles of maroon and stainless, while its interior boasts a whole host of noteworthies. There's a curved tan marble countertop, maroon and tan tiling throughout, maroon-topped yellow stools (eighteen of 'em), woodwork galore, and an entrance flanked by glass brick.

The Cutchogue is a diner with impressive roots, too. In 1933, one Olin Glover had a small wooden diner constructed on the site. Eight years later he converted this initial structure into a combination kitchen/back room, and went whole hog...purchasing a spanking new 1941 Kullman (Kullman Dining Car Company, Harrison, New Jersey) as the centerpiece of his operation. Five decades later it's still a centerpiece.

From a roadside architecture point of view, August 4, 1955 most definitely ranks as a banner day in the life of **DEPEW** (4 miles E of Buffalo). That's the day **ROBERT'S RESTAURANT**

came to town. The structure - which, in spite of its name, is a full-fledged diner, manufactured by Silk City Diners in Paterson, New Jersey - was moved to the Buffalo suburb from the Garden State at an average of ten miles per hour and arrived complete with a state trooper escort. The original proprietor, who owned the diner from 1955 to 1965, was Robert Estes. Since 1965 it's

been owned and operated - and very nicely cared for - by Peter Sciolino. Located at 4870 Broadway/Route 20, Robert's exterior shines of stainless steel with blue and white trim, highlighted by a row of neatly trimmed shrubs. The interior carries through the same color scheme of stainless and bright blue and white. If it all sounds pleasant and cheerful, that's because it is.

Peter Sciolino looking cool beside the entrance to his Robert's Restaurant. How does Peter explain the "Sorry, We're Closed" sign directly beneath the "Open 24 Hrs." proclamation? "Easy," he laughs. "We just close."

Luella Wheeler beams for the camera.

A smallish gem is **WHEELER'S CONEY ISLAND DRIVE-IN**, 34 Oak Street/Routes 8 and 10, **DEPOSIT**. Established by Luella and Erwin Wheeler in 1948, the Drive-In served but soft ice cream and Hire's Root Beer ("We just about wore out the root beer barrel," Luella recalls.) the first year. In 1949 they added hot dogs. In 1950 came hamburgers and French fries. Five-sided, with a facade of simulated cement, the Coney Island retains its postwar forties' good looks. Part of its appeal, though, is Luella herself. She

beams as she remembers some of the luminaries that have stopped by...singer Tony Orlando, boxer Carmen Basilio, vocal group the McGuire Sisters. (Note: Wheeler's Coney Island is open from April to October and, as of July, 1990, had no sign that said either "Wheeler's" or "Coney Island." Look for a small white building with a partially-hidden giant ice cream cone - as well as the American flag flying high - on the roof.).

Now three and a half decades old, the **GREEN ACRES DRIVE-IN**,

Route 29, **DOLGEVILLE**, is a good-sized and good-looking wooden eat-in or take-out landmark. Naturally enough, it's painted a bright green. Owned by the Stewart family since 1959, the Green Acres featured carhops through the mid-sixties. Plus Ruth Stewart-Jaikin, who bought the business from her dad in 1987, tried bringing curb service back one night a week in 1989. "We had fifties' music; the kids had fun," but, Ruth is sad to say, the carhops had no real impact on business, so it's an idea that's back on the backburner again.

The Green Acres, the front of its menu, and one of its several menu boards. The drive-in's specialty is a Big Acre: a one-third pounder with lettuce, tomato, onion and mayonnaise.

*If you're on Suffolk County's South Shore and in the mood to feast your eyes on a gas station that could only be described as adorable...head to **EAST MORICHES**, and the circa 1930s' ATLANTIC SERVICE STATION that's to be found on the Montauk Highway/Suffolk County Route 80, corner of North Paquatuck Avenue. It's a little white, red and gray - with half-moon cutout shutters, no less - beauty. Enhancing it further is the picket fence - also painted white, red and gray - that sets off the station's beguiling lawn. All in all, they don't often make them as appealing as this.*

The good citizens of Hawley, Pennsylvania need wonder no more: the polar bear that long adorned their now-defunct Polar Bear Restaurant is safe and sound and happy in **ELMIRA**. Made of heavy-duty fiberglass, he stands tall on the roof of the *MAPLE LAWN DAIRY BAR*, Lower Maple Avenue/Route 427. He's undoubtedly the best-dressed bear in either state, too. He has a summer outfit of shorts, top, and sunglasses, while in the winter he dazzles in a red scarf and red hat. (To be honest, however, it must have been between seasons the day I was there: Elmira's favorite bear was wearing but a birthday suit!). Dressed up or not, though, the Maple Lawn Bear is a splendid example of roadside allure. He's handsome, and he's large. How large? "Well, my husband has to stand on a ladder to put his hat on," relayed the restaurant's (and the bear's) owner, Mina DeRenzo. "And my husband's a good six feet tall."

*Want to feast your eyes on a twenty-foot tall, sixty-year old good-looking specimen of a duck? If so, just make your way to Route 24 in **FLANDERS** (6 miles SE of Riverhead) where you're sure to be enchanted by the BIG DUCK.*

The brainchild of one Martin Mauer, who wanted an eye-catching retail outlet for his Riverhead-area duck farm, the Duck was constructed by brothers Bill and Jack Collins in 1931. With experience as stage and prop designers, the brothers crafted a frame of wood and galvanized wire, and then covered it with four layers of white concrete.

They obviously knew what they were doing: six decades and two moves later the Collins' creation still stands as dashing as ever. Its future looks bright ahead, too. Suffolk County officials envision the not-too-distant day when they will create a museum devoted to commercial structures of the recent past; along the lines of the Henry Ford Museum in Deerfield Village, Michigan...but outdoors. You can most likely guess what's planned as the museum's main attraction. The Big Duck, of course!

Crocetta's Service: a touch of Tudor in Gloversville.

"They always figured that if it didn't work out as a gas station it could be a house." So explained Alex Dickson, proprietor of what is yet a gas station, and a treasure of a one. Built in 1937, what is now *DICKSON'S ATLANTIC*, 7995 West State Street, **GASPORT**, is probably best described as a white clapboard, with red and black trim, Tudor A-frame. A nice touch is the hanging plants that Alex, who's owned the station since 1965 and clearly has great pride in it, has spaced around the front of the station. Yes, there is a gas station in Gasport... and it's a treasure of a one.

South Street in **GLENS FALLS** is a small roadside haven. There's *PETER'S DINER*, 36 South, a homey luncheonette decorated with Reading Phillies and Glens Falls White Sox and the like pennants; the *NEW WAY LUNCH*, 54 South, which proclaims itself "King of the Hotdogs," has pressed tin roofing and walls, and has been serving up dogs since the 1920s; and a nice old neon sign that hangs over the entrance to the *IDEAL* (nee Falls) *DINER*, 60 South.

One of upstate's handsomer gas stations is undoubtedly *CROCETTA'S SERVICE*, on the corner of East Fulton Street and Thompson Avenue in **GLOVERSVILLE**. Constructed of stucco, with a color scheme of gray and red and a well-cared-for Spanish tile roof, Crocetta's is a delightful example of 1930s' Tudor charm.

Also in Gloversville, on South Main Street, is the *GLOVERSVILLE PALACE DINER*. Although its exteri-or (apart from its ancient neon "LUNCH" sign) is hum-drum at best, the Gloversville Palace's interior is largely original and features a marble counter and a spiffy tile floor. What's also intriguing is a photo - it's hung on the side wall -that shows the day the diner came to town: when it was being delivered by the Jerry O'Mahony diner manufacturing company back in August of 1923.

Red and white - and bright! - are the colors of *CORNER ICE CREAM*, 3914 Carman Road/corner of Routes 20 and 146, **GUILDERLAND** (10 miles W of Albany). Open from the first day of spring until late October, the stand began life as a Carvel in 1948, is now a rather striking concrete, wood, and glass (lots of glass) landmark owned by Ed and Ann Draiss. Ed's proud of the fact that soft ice cream has been served on the site for forty-two years. I would be, too.

It is no easy trick to describe *SLO JACKS DRIVE-IN*, 212 West Montauk Highway/Suffolk County Route 80, **HAMPTON BAYS**. Constructed circa 1960 and originally named The Bays, Slo Jacks is a large maroon and white tile structure surrounded by oodles of glass. "Futuristic," "sleek," "stylish" are all words that come to mind. Most dramatic of all are its huge blue and red neon arches. There are two of them, one on either side of the restaurant. Impressive by day, the twin arches are that much more so by night. John Balzer, who's owned Slo Jacks with his brother Tom since 1979, couldn't be prouder of them. "When you round the corner at night," he delights in describing, "it's almost eerie. Especially if it's a foggy night. It's like a magnet." (Note: Slo Jacks is open seven days a week from April until mid-November. It is closed the remainder of the year.).

Present-day Delights

The Wine List leads off with Quail Ridge Chardonnay ($27.50 a bottle/ $9.00 a glass) and the menu features the likes of Blackened Swordfish and Veal a la Rosa. Meatloaf is noticeably absent. **THE SILVER SPOON**, 301 Halstead Avenue, **HARRISON**, has gone upscale. Born Cappy's Diner circa 1940, the structure was for many years the Chinatown Diner. "A real greasy spoon," is how thirty-year old Brian Peroni describes it in those years. Brian, his wife Anne Marie, and his brother-in-law Chris McGovern, bought the Chinatown in 1985 and converted it into the cafe it is today. The handsome exterior - stainless with wide maroon vertical stripes - they left untouched. In fact, a "Diner" sign still hangs above the entrance. But it's there mostly for sentiment. Explained Brian: "If we take it down, we can't put it back. It's a town ordinance." The interior, however, is a different story. Modeled after Manhattan's well-known Empire Diner, it's heavy on pink and black, has lots of stainless, and plenty of neon, too. The back section, added onto the original diner, is built along the lines of a greenhouse. Call the Silver Spoon stunning, call the Silver Spoon obtrusive... but call it a good-looking former diner that's found new life pleasing a new generation of taste buds.

What is now **SULLIVAN'S DINER**, 151 Old Ithaca Road, **HORSEHEADS**, began life as Vic's Diner, in Elmira, in 1941. A Silk City, it was purchased by Arthur and Frances Sullivan and moved the half-dozen or so miles to Horseheads in October of 1975. After installing a new grill, building a basement for it, and, of course, re-christening it Sullivan's Diner, the Sullivans re-opened the diner in February, 1976. Apart from the new grill, their goal was to leave everything as original as possible. They have succeeded admirably! There's a lovely all early-1940s' interior with a plentitude of wood, green and black tiling, and an abundance of stainless steel. The exterior shines with a green and stainless all-metal facade, set off with a pair of gold-colored awnings. On one awning is imprinted a bright red "Sullivan's; on the other, an equally bright red "Diner." Well-kept shrubbery and a mini-collection of old railroad cars (Arthur is quite a train buff.) behind the diner round out a tableau that's most pleasant indeed.

Moved from Elmira in 1975, Sullivan's is owned and operated by Arthur and Frances Sullivan, their sons Artie and Dick, and their daughter Mary Helen. As Frances put it, "It's a family affair."

What I like most about the **COLUMBIA DINER**, *717 Warren Street,* **HUDSON,** *are its big red neon exterior letters that spell out "Diner." Opened in October of 1946, the Columbia's interior, alas, has been modernized.*

There are a number of older diners in the Binghamton-Endicott-Johnson City Triple Cities' area (Danny's, and the Park Diner in Binghamton, and the Skylark in Vestal are all worthy of note.), but my favorite is the **RED ROBIN DINER**, 286 Main Street, **JOHNSON CITY**. Owned by Chris Anagnostakos since 1970, the Red

The Red Robin...
a favorite in the Triple Cities' Area.

Robin is a Mountain View (constructed by Mountain View Diners, Singac, New Jersey) that was moved to its present site in 1955. Before that, it stood on Conklin Avenue in Binghamton. Chris believes it was there, in Binghamton, for twenty years or so, and that it was always called the Red Robin. A large silver - with horizontal red lines - stainless queen, the Red Robin is topped off with a wonderful "Red Robin" (in red) and "Diner" (in blue) neon that also includes, of course, a several-foot tall robin with a bright red breast.

Also in Johnson City, just up from the Red Robin, at 300 Main Street, is another place that's well worth a stop. It's *TONY'S TEXAS HOTS*, a pint-sized eatery that features pressed tin roof and walls throughout, and a row of adorable red-topped, almost claw-foot, stools.

I wouldn't call Joseph Basher a legend. I'm sure very few people in **LANCASTER** (5 miles E of Buffalo) today even know who he is. I would, however, call him dedicated. Here's a man who constructed his own gas station ("Oh, I had a carpenter help me with it, too," he modestly relates.) in 1932, has spent his entire working life in it, and at age 87, is still working in it. Located at 5870 Broadway/Route 20, *BASHER'S SERVICE STATION* is a handsome smallish stone bungalow-

Joseph Basher's station in the summer of 1990. To see a shot of his then four-year old son "manning" the pumps in 1939, please turn to page 51. Those were the days when a station could sell more than one brand. Represented in the 1939 photo are Pease (a former western New York regional brand), Gulf, and Tydol. In his fifty-four years behind the pumps Joe (that's he on the right) has also purveyed Atlantic, Cities Service, and Kendall.

with-canopy station. Joseph stopped pumping gas in 1986, now operates as more-or-less a combination auto supply/general store.

So many people told me about Heid's - "Wait 'til you see Heid's"/ "You're going to love Heid's!!" - that I expected to be disappointed. We've all doubtless experienced that: what's touted as the moon turns out to be decidedly more like green cheese. No green cheese here, however. *HEID'S*, 305 Oswego Street/Onondaga Lake Parkway at Route 57, **LIVERPOOL**, is the real thing. Heid's roots go back well before the Automobile Age, to 1886. In that long-ago year, Anna and

Michael Heid established a restaurant and grocery store very close to the site of today's landmark. That structure was destroyed by fire in 1913, to be replaced with a restaurant/bar. As prohibition loomed, in 1917, the Heids decided to play it safe. They went into the hot dog business. They've been in it ever since.

The building - let's make that *the building* - that everyone raves about was constructed in 1933, modernized in 1938. It's worth raving about! It's colorful: red, yellow, black, blue and glass block all flowing together. It's dramatic: its high-towered entrance topped with "Heid's" in red neon is a sure traffic stopper. What surprised me, though, was

Present-day Delights

Heid's of Liverpool: now in its 104th year in the food business and, of far greater significance, its seventy-third year in the hot dog business. Owned and operated by Helen Heid Platner, granddaughter of Anna and Michael, Heid's is unquestionably the most talked about roadside landmark in central New York. It well deserves to be.

that I found myself likening the restaurant's classic lines to that of a ship...with the entrance tower as a smokestack, the windows (especially the round one) as portals, etc. Crazy, I know, but...

Heid's circa 1954: snappy-looking then and snappy-looking now.

LLOYD'S OF LOWVILLE,
Utica Boulevard/Routes 12 and 26,
LOWVILLE, is a sterling example of a
good-looking diner built by other than
one of the diner manufacturing outfits.
It was built in 1939 for the Rogers &
Williams Oil Company, which owned a
gas station adjacent to the site of the
diner. They contracted with local
craftsmen Stuart Salzburg and Leonard
Terrillion. The result was the Lowville
Diner. The diner subsequently became
Todd's Diner when it was sold to Ralph
Todd in the early 1940s. It remained
Todd's until 1957 when Lloyd
Rasmussen purchased it and renamed
it Lloyd's Of Lowville. Since 1982 it's
been owned and operated by Blair
Sandri.

*Lloyd's exterior is a jaunty rust and
white in color, features a marvelous rooftop
sign that's black and yellow with pink neon
lettering that can only be described as a
knockout.*

In the late 1920s, the Pure Oil Company, then a major American petroleum company, developed a design for its stations that is still a standout today. Drive into **LYONS** and you'll see what I mean. On the corner of Geneva and Canal Streets there stands a striking thin red-brick English cottage-looking building with a steeply pitched blue clay tile roof, copper eaves, a bay window, and little gray shutters. That's the Pure Oil design. Today, however, the station is *JIM'S GULF*, James Pacello, III, proprietor. Jim is justly proud of it, and delighted that people so often comment on its beauty. (Note: there is another former Pure Oil station in nearby **FAIRPORT**. It's today an insurance office, but its good looks - and Tudor styling - are yet very much in evidence.).

"It would be un-American to give Walter's anything below a five-fork rating." So begins a review in the window of *WALTER'S*, 937 Palmer Avenue, **MAMARONECK** (3 miles NE of New Rochelle). It's true. Walter's is that much of an institution. Founded by Walter Warrington in 1919, the business was intitially located on the Boston Post Road. But in 1928 the move was made to Palmer Avenue. Walter's has been here ever since. What

brings people to the stand (the line at lunchtime is quite amazing!) is, of course, its hot dogs, the secret of which lies in the mustard-relish sauce. But I, at least, like to think people also come because Walter's is such a neat-looking place. Picture, if you will, a pagoda-shaped building, tan, brown, and black in color, with a sweeping green Spanish-tiled roof, and a large hanging sign on which "Walter's" is spelled out in - why not? - hot dogs. There's a wonderfully-inviting tree-shaded picnic grove next to the pagoda. And picture it all so well-kept that it appears as if it could've been built yesterday. That's Walter's!

Walter's as it appeared in 1931 and as it appeared in August of 1990. The sign has changed, the trees have grown fuller and, of course, the cars are different. Most everything else has remained the same. (P.S. That's Walter's founder Walter Warrington standing with hands on hips in the 1931 photograph.).

Walter's: Westchester's tribute to the hot dog. Walter, himself, retired in 1952, leaving the business - and the grill - to his two sons, Art and Gene. Art has since retired, too. Today the landmark is in the very capable hands of Gene. There's even talk of franchising Walter's, using the green pagoda-shaped roof as a trademark.

The years and the elements have taken a toll, but the once quite colossal marquee for the SUNSET DRIVE-IN THEATRE, 111 Church Street/Route 31, MIDDLEPORT (14 miles E of Lockport), still has a lot of luster left. Owned by the Stornelli family since its inception in 1950, the Sunset's marquee - actually more a sign - is neon-lighted with multi-colored arrows and, naturally enough, a bright orange sunset.

Behind its crisp - but not really noteworthy - yellow and green exterior, the *ANOTHER ROADSIDE ATTRACTION DINER*, Route 199, MILAN (6 miles E of Red Hook), pleases with a marvelously bright red and white interior. Built in 1949 by local carpenter/entrepreneur Roy Knapp as the Taconic Diner, it had gone through several changes in ownership, was in rather rundown condition when purchased by husband and wife team George Carrothers and Nancy Austin in 1988. With George overseeing restoration and Nancy overseeing the menu, the Another Roadside Attraction *has* become an attraction. And a success.

Some diners are a joy to behold on

the outside. Some diners are a joy to behold on the inside. *McBRIDE'S NEWARK DINER*, 246 East Union Street/Route 13, NEWARK, is both. Picture an exterior of bright yellow-with-deep-red-trim shiny porcelainized-metal, dark green awnings, a row of shrubs (punctuated with a *Democrat and Chronicle* machine on one side; a *Times-Union* on the other), and a dramatic red-on-white "Newark Diner"

sign overlooking it all. Inside there's a continuation of the yellow porcelainized-metal, lots of wood trim, a yellow barrel roof, and an unusual glass cabinet counter. Constructed by Sterling Diners of Merrimac, Massachusetts in 1937, the Newark Diner has always been on its current site. Present proprietors are Betty and Jim McBride, who purchased it in 1986, and who really enjoy being in the diner business.

Jim McBride cooking up an order of bacon.

"Pancakes/ALL-U-CAN-EAT/$1.25" heralds a large sign on one side of the diner, touting the McBrides' Monday night special. Does it do well? "It sure does," Jim assured me. "But Thursdays we have all-you-can-eat-spaghetti...which is even bigger."

Present-day Delights

When Tony Iliadis, then nineteen years old, saw the *FREEHOLD GRILL*, 59 East Main Street, **FREEHOLD**, being delivered and put in place by the Jerry O'Mahony company in June of 1947 did he ever dream he'd end up owning it? "No, not really," is his answer. But he did. In 1963 he and two friends, Mike DeCare and Jimmy Mageros, purchased what has become an institution in Freehold. Then, in 1970, Tony bought out his two partners and became sole proprietor. Most recently Tony has turned ownership over to his three sons, Pete, Elias, and Tommy. But the diner is still called Tony's Freehold Grill, and Tony's still the man (see page 97) at the grill.

The interior of Tony's Freehold Grill shines in hues of mauve, maroon, and rose. Plus, of course, there's tons of shiny stainless. The exterior is a crisp stainless and black. Perched high above the entrance is the neon lover's bonanza that's pictured here: eight feet or so of red and green and yellow. It's a dandy!

Max's has been owned and operated, since September of 1989, by Manuel Campos and Eduardo Rodas. Manuel had owned a local bar, but thought the diner/bar would be a better business. So far he's not sorry he made the switch.

Long live ***MAX'S GRILL***! Manufactured right in Harrison by the Kullman Dining Car Company, Max's, 731 Harrison Avenue, **HARRISON**, possesses one of the most winsome facades to be found. Anywhere. Glowing in porcelainized metal and embellished with an abundance of block lettering ("Max's Grill," "Ladies Invited," and "Table Service"), Max's reputedly dates to the 1920s. It has aged well. Its colors of dark red and pale yellow undoubtedly turn as many heads now as they did sixty years ago.

Max's interior is nothing to sneeze at, either. Original are the white metal grill hood, tan marble countertop, green and white floor tiling, and wooden storage cabinets. Not original is the way the diner entwines with an adjoining bar/pool hall. It's an interesting marriage.

JULE'S SERVICE DINER is a new kid on the block on Main Street/Route 9N in **BOLTON LANDING** (15 miles N of Glens Falls). But it's a new kid with a history, dating back to 1946 when it was manufactured by the Worcester Lunch Car Company of Worcester, Massachusetts. Stops along the way since its manufacture have included Providence, Rhode Island (as Mancini's Service Diner), Plainville (as Don's Diner) and North Attleborough (Eddie & Myle's Diner), Massachusetts. In 1988 it was purchased by partners Ike Wolgin and Henry Caldwell and moved to Bolton Landing. It opened for business at its new home on June 23, 1990, under the capable proprietorship of Dan and Julie Gillman. Julie, for whom the diner is re-named, fairly bubbles when she talks about their plans. A self-described "nostalgia freak," her goal is to transform Jule's Service into a "traditional 1940s' atmosphere." From what I can see, Julie's well on her way.

There is but one word that aptly describes Jule's Service Diner. That one word is gorgeous. Ike and Henry - with a lot of help from their friends - have thoroughly restored what was a gem to begin with. The interior glistens from top to bottom. There's mahogany woodwork throughout, oak and mahogany tables and chairs, fourteen blue-topped stools, tiling of blue, black and white, and a wonderful bright blue roof. The exterior is likewise a knockout: gleaming blue porcelainized metal with the words "Service" and "Booth Service" baked in.

The location is significant, too: it was the home of Bill Gate's Diner from 1949 until 1980. Gate's Diner is now at the Adirondack Museum in Blue Mountain Lake, awaiting restoration and eventual display. When it was moved, it opened a little piece of available land in the heart of Bolton Landing. What better way to have replenished that little piece of land than with a "new" diner?!

Open from mid-April until Labor Day, Mac's Drive-In is celebrating its thirtieth birthday in 1991. Originally located closer to downtown Waterloo, it was moved - via wide, wide flatbed - to its present site in 1967.

Don't try telling Raymond MacDougal, co-proprietor (with his brother, Gerald and their wives, Vera and Cathy) of *MAC'S DRIVE-IN*, 511 Waterloo-Geneva Road/Routes 5 and 20, **WATERLOO**, that the carhop/curb service business isn't what it used to be. "You gotta come back on a Friday or Saturday night," he beamed when friend Jim Starkman and I stopped by on a Wednesday eve. Actually, Mac's is a three-part affair. Closest to the Waterloo-Geneva Road

is a large square structure distinguished by the immense number of glass panels that comprise its walls on three sides. Weather permitting, the glass panels slide open, affording an open air effect in what is Mac's eat-in area. Atop this section is a rather nifty bright red and white 1950s'-type Richardson Root Beer sign. Next in line, further back from the road, is a white and red building that showcases an ice cream take-out window (that's on the outside; inside there's the

kitchen). Last comes the most intriguing part: the curb service area. There are two bays or runs, both eighty-five feet long, enough room for a total of sixty-four cars at any one time. "By 5:00 on Fridays and Saturdays both runs are full...and they stay that way," Ray beamed again. What I especially appreciated were the carhops' outfits: snappy red plaid skirts and caps and white blouses. Curb service is alive and well in Waterloo!

Service with a smile: Mac's Drive-In carhops Rebecca and Jeanette.

Give me the moon over Hanover: the Tropical Treat's rather wondrous neon gleams under the appreciative eye of a summer moon.

CRABBS TROPICAL TREAT, Route 94, **HANOVER**, lives up to its name: it is a treat. Opened in 1953 as an ice cream-only stand, two runways were added for carhop service in 1960. The original structure is white and features an inviting cone-shaped neon on its roof. The runways, with space for twenty cars and with a Teletray machine in each space for easy ordering, are canopied, resplendent in freshly painted green and white, and are, of course, what give the Tropical Treat its good old-fashioned curb service look.

Crabbs has been and remains truly a family affair. Begun by Clinton Crabb, it has been owned and operated by his sister and brother-in-law, Mary

and Maurice "Ike" Myers, since 1966. Waiting in the wings is the next generation of owners, Mary and Ike's three daughters, Darla, Donna, and Debra. All three work at the Treat; all three look forward to eventually being able to call it their own.

The Tropical Treat and what Ike calls his "Treatmobile," a bright red 1940 Ford panel truck that he restored in 1984, and that sports the Tropical Treat ice cream cone logo on its side.

Darla carhopping it. The Treat's specialty is its Fat Boy... twin beef patties, melted cheese, lettuce, onions, pickles, and the Treat's own special dressing, all served on a three-layer sesame bun. If it sounds like something you might get at the golden archs, as Ike laughs, it is... but the Tropical Treat had it in the Hanover area long before Mickey D's arrived on the scene.

It looks a little hokey - as if it belongs in California or Florida rather than the Keystone State - but that's part of its charm. It's the rather dazzling marquee for the **GARDEN DRIVE-IN THEATRE**, Route 11, **PLYMOUTH TOWNSHIP** (seven miles east of Shickshinny). Set atop a white cement block structure, the marquee itself is fifteen feet in length and six feet in height, with "Garden Drive-In" lighted in red neon and a large eye-catching palm tree standing tall on the sideline.

Constructed circa 1955 by the theatre's initial proprietor, Theodore Cragle, the marquee - and, for that matter, the entire theatre - was saved from extinction several years ago through the care and concern of the area's residents. In 1986, Nelson Fey, owner of Calex Trucking, Inc., bought the theatre and the land it occupied with the full intention of leveling everything and building a new terminal for his company's trucks. But, as Doug Barbacci, Nelson Fey's son-in-law, recounted it to me, there was such a public outcry ("We got phone calls like you wouldn't believe... begging us not to close.") that it was decided to keep the theatre open. What's especially heartwarming is that after a slow start the theatre - open Friday, Saturday, and Sunday - is going great guns. The area not only rallied to save the Garden; they're rallying to give it business. Plenty of business. To again quote Doug: "Now we'll never shut it down."

Circle Drive-In Theatre, Dickson City, Pennsylvania.

For the story of the Circle Drive-In Theatre and its marvelous marquee, please see page 141.

Walter's: what a nice way to close out our in-color section. For the story of Westchester County's best-known contribution to roadside architecture, please turn to pages 118-119.

Walter's
937 Palmer Avenue
Mamaroneck, New York

*"My" cabin when I visited <u>OSWEGO</u>. Isn't it adorable? It's one of a group of circa 1930 little abodes that call **SUNSET CABINS** home. Located on Washington Boulevard, the cabins live up to their name: they're almost right on the water... and the sunset over Lake Ontario is really something to see.*

Among the most flourishing drive-in theatres in the state is the **SILVER LAKE DRIVE-IN**, Castile Road/Route 39, **PERRY** (24 miles SE of Batavia). Dating back to 1949, the Silver Lake is part of a complex, open April to October, that includes a restaurant, an ice cream parlor, and a miniature golf course. The theatre features impressively-landscaped grounds, a playground, and ambitious-minded management on the part of the owners, Jacob and Josie Stefanon and their son Rick. Rick is planning several special events, including an Antique Auto Night, and can rattle off a host of most successful features that have played the Silver Lake in the past few years. ("Disneys always do well: when we have Disney the playground is so full of kids you wouldn't believe it!"). Rick was also generous enough to lend me material from the theatre's grand opening in September of 1949. Reproduced on the following page is a sampling of that material.

Silver Lake
Drive-in Theatre
CASTILE ROAD — ONE MILE SOUTH OF PERRY

Shows at 7 and 9 p.m.

FRIDAY, SATURDAY   Sept. 23, 24

"BODY and SOUL"
With John GARFIELD, Lillian PALMER

SUNDAY, MONDAY   Sept. 25, 26

"VARIETY GIRL"
All Star Cast including Bob HOPE and Bing CROSBY

TUES., WED., THUR.   Sept. 27, 28, 29

'IT HAPPENED ON 5th AVENUE'
Don DeFORE, Ann HARDING

FRIDAY, SATURDAY   Sept. 30, Oct 1

"DESERT FURY"
IN TECHNICOLOR
with Elizabeth Scott, John Hodiak, Bert Lancaster

Program Includes
Short Subjects Every Night

Silver Lake
Drive-in Theatre
PERRY-CASTILE ROAD   PHONE 101-R

Western New York's Newest and Best Equipped Drive-In
ROUTE 39 ONE MILE SOUTH OF PERRY
TWO SHOWS NIGHTLY 7 and 9 P.M. — CLEAR OR RAIN

FRIDAY, SATURDAY   Sept. 30, Oct 1

"DESERT FURY"
IN TECHNICOLOR
with Elizabeth Scott, John Hodiak, Bert Lancaster

SUNDAY, MONDAY   Oct. 2-3

"COPACABANA"
with Groucho Marx and Carman Miranda

TUES., WED., THURS.   Oct. 4-5-6

"PERILS OF PAULINE"
— IN TECHNICOLOR —
Betty Hutton, John Lund and Wm. Damarest

Children under 12 free. Adults 50 cents. A speaker in every car—Clear or Rain—Don't change your clothes, come as you are. Bring the children—no baby sitting problem. Smoke, talk, relax in your own car. Free to mothers—bottle warming at the refreshment stand where hot coffee, hot dogs, hot chocolate, popcorn, etc., are sold.

You'll Enjoy the "Stars Under the Stars"

You are cordially invited
to be a guest at the private

Pre-View

of the Silver Lake Drive-in Theatre

Thursday, September 22, 1949

at 7:30 p.m.

"Stars Under the Stars"

The Silver Lake was launched by initial proprietor Harry K. Martin (the Stefanons purchased it in the mid-1960s) on September 23, 1949. Admission was 50¢ per person, with children under 12 admitted free. Management boasted "Western New York's Newest and Best Equipped Drive-In"; provided free bottle warming; promised "You'll Enjoy the Stars Under the Stars."

"What's it like working in a building old enough to be your grandfather?" I asked sixteen-year old Pete Glennon as he filled my car with super unleaded. His first reaction: that it's a pain in the ...; that it's always needing work; that it's drafty as .... in the winter. But then, knowing my "mission," he beamed and added, "It's worth it though; it's a nice little place." And, indeed, it is. Now an *ATI* station, the smallish wooden white-with-green-trim structure located at the corner of Church Street/Route 199 and Pioneer Drive in **PINE PLAINS** (16 miles E of Kingston) has filling station roots that go back to the late 1920s/early 1930s, when initial proprietor Ike Kilmer started pumping Texaco.

"It's a nice little place."

PLATTSBURGH features two places of note. *CLAIRE & CARL'S,* Lake Shore Road/Route 9 south, is an attractive little 1942 structure, white with maroon awnings, a glass block front, and a Texas Red Hots sign that's hard to miss. Open from May until September, with carhop service.

Just down Lake Shore Road is *NITZI'S*. Built in 1945, the present structure - successor to a much smaller stand ("Nitzi" is a bastardized version of a Jewish term for "little one," explained Lila Rabin, widow of long-time former proprietor Jack Rabin) - was *the* curb service restaurant in the Plattsburgh area in the late forties and the fifties. "I can recall when we had fifteen to eighteen carhops working on Saturdays and Sundays," reminisced Lila. Now owned by Arnie Pavone, Nitzi's is not the carhop haven it used to be. But it still offers limited curb service...plus it claims to be the home of the Michigan Red Hot. What's a "Michigan Red Hot?" Well, relayed Arnie - making it clear that it's unique to the area - it starts with an extra large bun that you steam; then comes a hot dog; then you add meat sauce atop the bun; then you top it all with mustard

Carhop Melissa at Claire & Carl's

and onions. Zowie. "People come from all over to try it. Then they come back," promised Arnie. Having had one, I believe it!

A most inviting little cabin court is BLUE ANCHOR CABINS, Route 28 north, POLAND (14 miles NE of Utica). Initially located in nearby Remson, the cabins were transported to their present site in the 1920s. There are seven of them - each white with blue trim and with its own gable - nestled in a grove of trees and backing on West Canada Creek.

The first diner to be listed on New York's Register of Historic Buildings. And the fourth diner* to be included on the National Register. Both honors - and they are very meaningful honors! - go to the *"HISTORIC" VILLAGE DINER*, 39 North Broadway/Route 9, **RED HOOK** (10 miles NE of Kingston). As is not unusual with a diner, the Village has had several lives. It was initially - from 1925 until 1928 - located on Route 9 in the Astor Flats section of

Rhinebeck. Its stay there, though, was to be shortlived: proprietor Lou DuBois passed away suddenly in 1928, and the diner was purchased by Bert Coons. A Red Hook resident, Coons moved the diner several miles up the road to its present location. There it remained until the Taconic State Parkway was completed through Dutchess County just after World War II. Sensing the opportunity for more business if he were near the parkway's intersection

with Route 199 in Lafayetteville, Coons relocated. The diner would most likely still be there except that business from people getting on and off the parkway was never as brisk as Coons hoped. So, circa 1957, he moved it one last time...back to where it had been in Red Hook.

While Bert Coons is the man responsible for moving the diner to Red Hook - not once, but twice! - the man (actually the couple: Arleen Harkins is as much a part of the team as Sam) responsible for the magnificance of today's Village Diner is Sam Harkins. Sam and Arleen used to eat at the diner quite often. Then, in January of 1984, they noticed a *Pennysaver* ad announcing that it was for sale. As relayed by Sam: "I was tired of all the travel in my job (with the Kraft dairy group); we looked at the diner that weekend; put in an offer the next weekend... and three weeks later I was in the kitchen."

* The others are the Modern Diner, Pawtucket, Rhode Island; the Blue Moon Diner, Gardner, Massachusetts; and Mickey's Diner, St. Paul, Minnesota.

"...and three weeks later I was in the kitchen": Sam Harkins

What makes the "Historic" Village Diner (that really is its name, with quotes surrounding the word historic) special is both its interior and its exterior. The exterior features fluted stainless with a horizontal yellow and green band, and a dramatic green-with-red-neon-lettering rooftop "DINER" sign. The interior sparkles with black and dark lime green tiling, a yellow roof, and an abundance of stainless steel. Even the original lime green and black Seth Thomas clock is in place.

"The Village Diner is a well-preserved example of the 'golden age' of the roadside dining car. Its shiny, banded metal exterior and monitor roof recall the sleekness of a railroad car and reflect the popular interest in streamlined design in the 1920's and 1930's. Typical of early-twentieth century roadside architecture, the diner is as much a sign as a building, a readable structure whose function and purpose is obvious from a moving automobile. Surviving essentially intact from its date of construction, the diner maintains associations with that period of diner history as well as features that represent important transitional points in the evolution of the type and its function in the roadside development of the area. The Village Diner is a rare survivor and a landmark in the architectural and transportation history of northern Dutchess County."

Documentation, Village Diner National Register of Historic Places Inventory-Nomination Form

A Silk City (manufactured by the Paterson Vehicle Company, Paterson, New Jersey), the diner was initially named the Halfway Diner because its location in Rhinebeck was halfway between New York City and Albany. Sam had to strip away "about nine coats of paint" to get down to the original porcelainized-metal band and Halfway Diner lettering. The results well justified the effort.

Patron Jonathan Buchwalter of Wappingers Falls, New York: when you're four years old it's fun to peek out of a diner's railroad-style windows. (When you're thirty-four or forty-four it's fun, too!).

What do you do when you visit an area and like it...but have a going business back home, hundreds of miles away? You transfer it, of course. Or at least that's what the Terry Stoner family did. Operators of a successful barbeque restaurant, Spicy's, in Rochester, they visited relatives on Long Island in the mid-1970s. They liked Long Island; so much so that they moved there in 1977.

With them came the business. To house it they bought the Twin Diner, 225 West Main Street, **RIVERHEAD**, changed its name to *SPICY'S*...and have been barbequing happily ever after.

"The Spicy Girls" - as Josie Stoner kiddingly dubbed herself and her co-workers - in front of Spicy's. That's, from left to right, Denise Edwards, Josie Stoner, and Elsie Phelps. Although it's been a barbeque restaurant for its last thirteen years, the former Twin Diner still looks like a diner. And that's good.

"We're hot. We're the hottest thing in town," Bob Malley, proprietor of the **HIGHLAND PARK DINER**, 960 South Clinton Avenue, **ROCHESTER**, told me as I chatted with him early on a Thursday morning. It's easy to see why: the Highland Park is striking in looks, known for quality food, is spotless... and is trendy. Old (some original/some reproduction) ads and signs line the walls; a heavily lime green and black and stainless color scheme bedazzles; maroon-topped stools (that came out of an old Woolworth's) charm; a yellow barrel roof oversees things. Bob, who loves old things and has restored many an antique auto ("...but this, the diner, is my biggest restoration."), is responsible for it all. In 1986, he bought what was a rapidly-disintegrating former diner from the folks at OTB, who had been operating it as an off-track betting parlor since 1976. Bob had no choice

Bob Malley: "We're hot."

but to gut the vast majority of the inside (although, fortunately, the original walls and ceilings were salvageable). He's done a magnificent job.

The exterior had fared better than the interior: most of it is original, dating back to 1948 when the diner, then known as Dauphin's Superior Diner, arrived on the scene. It, too, is striking, with porcelainized-metal panels of yellow and green. The one real change - and it's a dramatic one - was the addition of a twenty-eight foot pink (in neon) and green (in neon) and black sign that spells out "Highland Park Diner" across the top of the entrance-way. It cost $8,000 to have the sign crafted by local neon expert Gene Roth, but, as Bob smiles, it's been "$8,000 well spent."

A Diner Reborn

   Highland Park Diner, Rochester. Constructed by the little-known diner manufacturing firm of Orleans Dining Car Company in Albion (the county seat of Orleans County), New York, the Highland Park has gone through several lives. It was a diner from 1948 to 1974; vacant in 1975 and 1976; an OTB parlor from 1976 to 1986; a reborn diner from 1986 on.

Picture shiny blue and yellow porcelainized-metal facing, a pair of well-endowed windows highlighted by pink neon strips (with a curlycue on the bottom!), plus a bright red neon "Restaurant" sign, too... and you have the *MAIN STREET RESTAURANT*, 244 Main Street, <u>SAUGERTIES</u>. Owned by sisters Catherine Coby and Natalie MacLarey, the Main Street's exterior is a tribute to its 1920s' heritage. The only problem is that, while Catherine likes things just fine the way they are, sister Natalie isn't so sure. She thinks maybe they should "modernize." What a shame that would be.

A little bit of old Mexico in central New York: that's *DEDELL'S MOTEL*, Route 5, <u>SHERRILL</u> (17 miles W of Utica). Opened by Richard and Vivian Dedell just after World War II, and now owned by Lee and Rose White, the motel sports an all pink and white color scheme, a central stucco section that's complete with balcony and an imitation Spanish tile roof, miniature palm trees, etc., etc. Sound dreadful?

Actually, it's not. In fact, it all comes together rather well. You may feel you're seventeen miles west of Mexico City rather than seventeen miles west of Utica...but what the heck. Why not?!

Originally the Palace Diner and located in Albany, what is now WOLFF'S DINER, Route 4, <u>STILLWATER</u> (12 miles N of Troy), was moved to its present site circa 1970. For many years it was known as Carol's Diner, became Wolff's in September of 1989 when it was purchased by 23-year old Dave Wolff. Fresh out of Johnson and Wales College, Dave just wanted to own a restaurant. The diner features a blue and stainless facade and a sign that promises "Great Coffee." Indeed, Dave proudly told me, he does get many a compliment on the coffee. "We use our own well water," he summed up.

MARIO'S LITTLE GEM DINER, 832 Spencer Street, <u>SYRACUSE</u>, is not little (although its interior is much less spacious than its exterior would suggest), but it does possess many of the qualities of a gem. And it is owned by a man named Mario. A circa 1950 Fodero (manufactured by the Fodero Dining Car Company, Newark, New Jersey), the diner was purchased by Mario Biasi in 1982. Prior to that it was known as Hank McCall's Little Gem. What I like most about it is how all sorts of bright and perhaps otherwise busy colors come together to form a most alluring interior. There is the pink and turquoise counter base, the pink ceiling, turquoise walls, maroon stools, multi-colored drapes, and a mirror that runs the entire length of the ceiling. There's also, of course, the de rigueur stainless. In fact, there's an abundance of it. Sounds as if it's too much, I know, but it all seems to work well in total. Stop by sometime (Mario's is open every hour of every day of the year!) and enjoy a helping of the house specialty, Frittata (which is a blending of eggs, onions, ham, potatoes and broccoli, and translates to "all mixed up" in English, I learned from Joe Biasi, Mario's son), and see if you don't concur.

Present-day Delights

I'm always at least slightly suspicious of "World Famous" places that I've never heard of. But something made me go into the **FAMOUS LUNCH** ("World Famous Hot Dogs"), 111 Congress Street, **TROY**. I'm glad I did. Inside is a delightful setting. When I commented to co-owner Kay Vasiliades - who's delightful herself - that it appears as if nothing much has been touched since the eatery's founding in 1932, she laughed and responded, "It hasn't." There are a half-dozen wooden booths, sixteen stools, green and white tiles, and a well-worn counter top. (Well-worn as it is, Kay and her brother-in-law and co-proprietor Steve Vasil have no plans to replace the top. They feel "it has character." They're so right!).

The "World Famous" - which was added in 1958 - came about in rather heartwarming fashion. A soldier by the name of Gordon Gundrum, from nearby Grafton, was stationed at the U.S. Embassy in Moscow. In an interview he was asked what he missed most from back home. His reply: "Hot dogs from the Famous Lunch." The folks at Famous Lunch got wind of this and, in August of 1958, made special arrangements to fly a shipment of their distinctive dogs, packed in dry ice, to Moscow. The wire services picked the story up and, voilà, the Famous *was* suddenly world famous.

Also in Troy, at 40 Third Street, is the **PURITAN TEA ROOM**. In business since 1922, the Puritan retains a goodly share of its original flavor.

UNADILLA (15 miles SW of Oneonta) calls itself "The Village Beautiful." It's an apt nickname. Adding to the beauty is a pair of roadside notables. Foremost is the **UNADILLA DINER**, 57 Main Street/Route 7, which is actually not one, but

The gang at the Unadilla: left to right, Jason Rude, Ray Wiswell, II, Mary Greene, and Mary's niece, Valarie McGraw.

two, diners. What is now the kitchen was Jay's Diner, a long-time fixture that sat perpendicular to Main Street. In 1954, a gentleman by the name of Al Braunstein had a then six-year old diner transported from Mineola, Long Island, and positioned it, lengthwise, in front of Jay's. The newly-"married" duo became today's Unadilla Diner. One important addition, that of a sizable front "porch," was made circa 1970. Built by Master Diners, of Pequannock, New Jersey, the Unadilla has a facade that features red and stainless steel-colored vertical stripes (as well as the porch, of course), while its interior features a warm maroon hue and a plentitude of stainless (Master's slogan was "Stainless Steel Used Throughout."). Presiding over it all is most personable Mary Greene, who purchased the diner from longtime owner (twenty-seven years!) Larry Henchey in December of 1985.

Also in Unadilla, about a mile west on Main Street/Route 7, is a natty little white-with-blue-trim **GULF STATION**. It's circa 1930 and nicely maintained. And, it's nice to be able to say, a brief chat with the owner indicates it's going to remain well-maintained: he recognizes the station's specialness.

It probably really isn't roadside, but the **CRYSTAL RESTAURANT** 87 Public Square, **WATERTOWN**, deserves every accolade it can get. Originally a taproom/saloon, the Crystal was remodeled into a restaurant when liquor went illegal in 1919. Not much has changed since. Etched-glass mirrors, a pressed tin roof, black and white inlaid tile, and finely-detailed walnut panels: all are still marvelously in place. Jests part-owner Leo DePhtereos: "We have a hundred year program: we remodel every one hundred years." The result is very, very pleasing indeed.

What's ninety feet long, has a fore and an aft, and has portals, too...and is permanently "docked" at the junction of Routes 5 and 26 in <u>VERNON</u> (14 miles W of Utica)? The answer is THE BOAT, a full-menu restaurant constructed in 1923 ("by two drunken sailors," one of the bar crowd interjected the day I was there) and owned by the Demma family since 1945. Built as a traffic stopper, the almost seventy-year old structure yet serves that purpose (try driving along Route 5 and missing it!)... but in a pleasing, rather that garrish, way. Quite simply, The Boat is an attractive boat, and a stop that's become somewhat of a central New York institution. As co-proprietor John Demma proudly phrased it: "We get generations and generations coming back."

The Texas Hot, Wellsville, features a 1921 facade set in a circa 1880 building that was once the home of the Lyric Theatre. To this day, in fact, it's difficult to miss the word "Lyric" etched into the sidewalk blocks immediately in front of the restaurant.

<u>WATERLOO</u>: please see page 124.

<u>WELLSVILLE's</u> North Main Street fairly dazzles in the glow of its rich and varied architectural styles. Among my favorite examples are the deco-influenced entranceway to the Lin-Ray Twin Theatre, the sign for the otherwise largely-modernized Modern Diner, and the exceedingly handsome Benezer Oil Company Building. The apex of it all, at least in my view, is the rather wondrous 1921 facade of *THE TEXAS HOT*, 132 North Main. Featuring bright green glass block, a more than fair share of stainless steel, and huge "Texas Hot" lettering - all punctuated by a circa 1930 red and green neon hanging sign - The Texas Hot is a gem. What's also well worthy

of note is that the same two families that began things seven decades ago are still the restaurant's owners and operators...and still having fun at it. Twenty-nine year old Mike Raptis clearly enjoys what he's doing. And he assured me that his partner, twenty-six year old Chris Rigas, does also. It was their grandparents, George Raptis and Jim Rigas, who founded The Texas Hot. (Note: after admiring the restaurant's exterior, be sure to venture inside as well. The original 1921 tin ceiling is still in place; there are sixteen gorgeous wooden booths; and there are, of course, the famed Texas Hots themselves. "Our success lies in our secret hot sauce recipe for the hots," Mike told me, adding, "Everyone who's ever lived here in Wellsville: whenever they come back to visit they come here first... then they go home.").

VOSS': A favorite in the Utica area since 1937.

"He loved ice cream," laughed Dorothy Voss when I asked what had inspired she and her late husband John to go into the ice cream stand business in 1937. Now, almost five and a half decades later, **VOSS'**, Oriskany Street/Route 5A and Cooper Avenue, **YORK-VILLE** (a stone's throw west of Utica), is still going strong. And it's still in the Voss family. And, perhaps most important of all, it's still doing business in its original building, a cozy-white-with-blue-trim structure topped with a twelve-foot or so tall milk bottle. Constructed of galvanized tin, it, too, has been on duty since 1937. "It was one of the first things we put up," Dorothy recalls. The

bottle was once outlined in neon. But no more. "That didn't prove practical," Dorothy further explained.

There is, though, an extant neon roof sign. And it's a beauty. Approximately sixteen feet side to side, it's red and white and features a hefty steaming hot dog (hot dogs, hamburgers et al were added to the ice cream line in 1950), as well as the words "Bar B-Q," "Franks," and "Home Made Ice Cream." (Note: Voss,' a don't miss when in the Utica area, is open from mid-April until the first of December.).

Also in Yorkville - in fact conveniently located right next door to Voss', at 107 Oriskany Street - is the

YORKVILLE DINER. Constructed in 1957, the Yorkville's spacious interior highlights an abundance of stainless steel and an apricot-hued roof. Its facade is also stainless, with what can best be described as bits and pieces of blue adornment. What I admire most is the diner's handsome - and large - "Yorkville Diner/Fine Food" neon and electric sign, located smack over the entrance. "Very bright," summed up the waitress on duty when I inquired about the sign's impact. "Wonderful waitresses," she summed up when I asked what brings customers to the Yorkville. She's probably right on both counts.

Pennsylvania

What's in a name? Plenty in the case of ANDERSON'S DINER, 922 Union Boulevard, ALLENTOWN. Although the diner itself has been largely remodeled, its sign, gloriously, has not been. It dates back to 1955 when what had been the Irving Street Diner became Anderson's.

Now approaching sixty years of age, the small but stately always-a-gas-station structure that houses ANSONIA GULF, Route 6, ANSONIA (8 miles W of Wellsboro), is still hanging in there, selling gas - two pumps - as well as basic groceries and Sunset ("Williamsport's Famous") Ice Cream. When it opened in 1933, gas was two gallons for 25¢.

Chances are you won't be overly impressed by the dark red metal facade of the *CONGRESS STREET DINER*, 16 Congress Street, **BRADFORD**. But step inside for a real treat: four lovely original booths, eleven original stools, and an openness and spaciousness not at all evident from the street. Built by Rochester Grills (of Rochester, New York) circa 1940, the Congress Street has been owned and operated by the dedicated trio of Rosa McAndrew, Juanita Delvelcchio, and Juan Domenech since 1979.

Bob Weisser is a World War II navy veteran. His diner, *BOB'S DINER*, 134 Lancaster Avenue/Route 462, **COLUMBIA** (12 miles W of Lancaster), reflects it. There's a ships bell clock - which chimes every half hour - over the entrance to the kitchen; there's a large model - which Bob built himself out of cardboard from egg crates - of the ship on which Bob served; the exterior is bedecked with miniature American flags. It's nice. And it lends a distinctive atmosphere to Bob's, a 1947 Mountain View (Mountain View Diners, Singac, New Jersey) that has eyecatching curved glass brick corners, blue and white checkerboard curtains, and an overall bright blue scheme.

Also in Columbia, on Route 462 east, is the *PROSPECT DINER*.

Located on the site of the former DD Diner, the circa 1950 Prospect is stainless and red and good-looking.

CONNEAUT LAKE: please see pages 144-145.

THE CUSTER CITY DRIVE-IN, Route 219, **CUSTER CITY** (3 miles S of Bradford), is your basic 1950's (it was constructed in 1955) glass-front-with-large-overhang ice cream/hamburger stand. It's more colorful than most, however (and most are quite colorful to start with!)... especially if you like turquoise. I do.

Now you have the time, now you have the temperature... with the quite spectacular marquee for the CIRCLE DRIVE-IN THEATRE, Scranton-Carbondale Highway/Route 6, <u>DICKSON CITY</u> (1 mile NE of Scranton). Original (or, almost all original: the time and temperature arm was added circa 1980) with the opening of the theatre in 1946, the marquee is twenty feet in length, approximately sixteen in height. It can be more than a little hypnotic, what with the round "Circle" flashing on and off in a beautiful lime green, the time and temperature constantly alternating, and the overall rainbow of color that's on display. Put it all together and the result: sheer magic.

Note: to view the Circle's marquee in full - and glorious - color, please turn to page 127.

Projectionist Angelo Dominick, left, and manager Bob Kaszuba, right. Between them they have eighty-three years at the Circle (add owner Michael Delfino with his twenty-four years, and you have a grand total of one-hundred and seven years at the drive-in!). Bob started at age eleven as a 50¢ per hour member of the clean-up crew. He advanced to usher, assistant manager, and is now manager. He vividly recalls the banner years back in the 1950s when it was routine to have 600-800 cars packed in for a show (now the total is more like 100-200) and the staff included a host of specialists: cashiers, ticket takers, window washers (yes, window washers!), and ushers (who'd guide you to your stall with the aid of a flashlight). Now it's the every-Sunday flea market that's the biggest revenue producer. Still, Bob clearly enjoys himself: he loves the theatre, his job, and the customers who come on out. His son, Bob, Jr., is now in his third year of working at the theatre, too.

The Circle Drive-In is open from late March until the end of November. Its landmark marquee, though, is "open" all year long: it's used for advertising during the winter months.

"The friends I've made. Customers who've become friends. We have people who come in here every day, twice a day. They're like family." That's the answer I got when I asked Lillian Atkin how she'd characterize her thirty-two years at **WOLFE'S DINER**, Route 15, **DILLSBURG** (12 miles SW of Harrisburg). Lillian and partner Bob Richwine bought Wolfe's, a 1954 Jerry O'Mahony (manufactured by Jerry O'Mahony company, Elizabeth, New

Lillian Atkin, her diner, and her sign.

Jersey) from original proprietor Paul Wolfe in 1958. They've never changed the name because people know it as Wolfe's; with two families there might be a problem as to whose name to use were they to change it; and, as Lillian admits, "It was too easy to keep the signs as they were." It's a blessing: while the diner itself is undeniably attractive both inside and out, it's the sizable red and yellow and green and white "Wolfe's Diner" neon sign out front that tickles my fancy the most. It's calculated to pull you in off the highway. It does!

A summer Sunday eve at the RED RABBIT DRIVE-IN ("Make The Red Rabbit A Habit"), Routes 22 and 322, <u>DUNCANNON</u> (15 miles NW of Harrisburg). It was 6:00 and it was mob city. I had a difficult time just finding a parking spot. Employing a host of carhops (that's Dayna Rash pictured here), the Red Rabbit began business in 1964, is an alluring red and white, and is open Friday, Saturday, and Sunday from February until November. And yes, it's the home of the Bunnyburger (a hamburger with cheese, bacon, tomato, lettuce, onions, and a special - and secret - sauce).

Jim and Betty Shepard, and a close-up of their Dinor sign. Their Union City Dinor is a Mulholland (manufactured by the P.J. Mulholland Company, Dunkirk, New York). Records indicate that it arrived in Union City in 1926. Jim and Betty bought it in March of 1990.

I'd heard about it: that in and around **ERIE COUNTY** the word "diner" is spelled "dinor." Still, when I came upon it for the first time - at *JIM AND BETTY'S UNION CITY DINOR*, West Main and High Streets, **UNION CITY** (20 miles SE of Erie) - I was somewhat taken aback. After almost two full days in the area, however, I found that I came to like it. "Dinor" came to look natural.

The question is how did the word come to be spelled with an "o" around Erie and only around Erie.

The answer is that no one really knows.

One theory - held by Jim and Betty Shepard of Jim and Betty's - is that it's just logical. As Betty explained it: "To me it makes sense. The 'dinor' should be the building; the 'diner' should be the one who dines." Sounds logical enough.

A second theory is that the spelling is somehow German. A check of three German-English dictionaries, however,

failed to disclose any German connection.

The third theory - the one that's most widely espoused - is simply that it's a misspelling. Terri Burleson of the *GREENVILLE DINOR*, 9-11 South Mercer Street/Route 58, **GREEN-VILLE** (22 miles SW of Meadville), holds this theory. "We don't know how to spell," she says flat out. Mary Wayne,

of the *LIGHTHOUSE DINOR*, Water Street/Routes 6 and 322, **CONNEAUT LAKE** (8 miles W of Meadville) puts it more bluntly: "There was just some dummy who didn't know how to spell, and everybody else went along."

Brian Butko, a western Pennsylvania historian who's a particular fan of diners/dinors, was my last hope. But he, too, has thus far concluded that no

*RUSS' DINOR, 2902 Buffalo Road/ Route 20, **WELSLEYVILLE** (½ mile E of Erie). Owned by Ron Russ, Russ' features a large "Russ' Dinor Restaurant" sign, with smiling chef, atop its roof. It's bright green, and it's a standout.*

Sign for the Greenville Dinor. The Greenville is a large yellow brick structure with a commanding overhang. It was here that the "German connection" was put forth.

Mary Wayne of the Lighthouse Dinor: "There was just some dummy who didn't know how to spell, and everybody else went along." The Lighthouse is a hand-crafted dinor, constructed by local carpenter George Berkey. It has been at its present site since 1940.

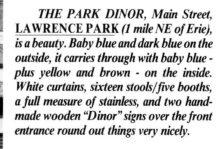

THE PARK DINOR, Main Street, LAWRENCE PARK (1 mile NE of Erie), is a beauty. Baby blue and dark blue on the outside, it carries through with baby blue - plus yellow and brown - on the inside. White curtains, sixteen stools/five booths, a full measure of stainless, and two hand-made wooden "Dinor" signs over the front entrance round out things very nicely.

one really knows the reason behind the dinor tradition in the northwest section of the state.

Whatever the reason - or lack of one - the spelling is unique. And I, for one, like it. Who says a "diner" can t be a "dinor?"

All Aboard

Perhaps the most intriguing dinor is the CROSSROADS, located at 101 Plum Street/Routes 6N and 99, in EDINBORO (15 miles S of Erie). A goodly number of diners/dinors are rumored to be former trolley cars. The Crossroads really is. It was car number 103, one of a two-car train constructed in 1913 and used to haul milk, coal, passengers and just about anything else that needed transporting on the old Northeastern Electric Service Company between Erie and Linesville. When train service ended in the late 1920s most of the rolling stock was junked or scrapped. Number 103 fared better: in early 1929 it was set on the corner where it still is today, remodeled, and opened - on May 30th - for business as an eating establishment.

Sixty-one years later it's still an eating establishment. Its exterior reminds me, at least, of a small white New England church. Once you enter, however, you might almost expect to hear someone announce "All aboard." That's how much the Crossroads maintains its feel of a trolley. And a gorgeous trolley, with leaded glass across its top, a rounded "front" and "rear," and a bright-white-with-gobs-of-turquoise color scheme.

All is not paradise in Edinboro, however. Sixty-five year old Andrew Mukina, who's owned the dinor since 1950, is ready to retire and there are no buyers in the offing. The fate of the Crossroads is, sad to say, uncertain.

After almost two full days I found myself liking "dinor." When, as I headed further from Erie and ran across my first spelling of the word - as I approached Mercer - in the more traditional manner, I was tempted to go in and ask the owner why he/she spelled it that way.

Sign for the *MERCER DINER* (a.k.a. Lucky's Diner), Route 58, MERCER.

It's been the Paoli Diner (from its origin there in 1929 until moved to Frazer in 1957), Cavy's Diner, Zit's Diner, Bob's Truck Stop, and Ethel's Diner. But now it's the *FRAZER DINER*, 189 West Lancaster Avenue/Route 30, **FRAZER** (18 miles W of Philadelphia), and it's quite exquisite. Built by the Jerry O'Mahony company, the Frazer's interior attributes include a black marble countertop, tiling in various shades of black, red, maroon and gray, an original Jerry O'Mahony clock set into the panel above the counter, and maple woodwork throughout. The woodwork alone is worth the trip. There are also sliding glass windows - which still open - to re-inforce the overall rail car look. The Frazer's exterior is white and maroon with "Frazer Diner" in bold black script (set off by a bed of marigolds in full bloom the day I visited in late August).

HANOVER: *to read all about the home of the Fat Boy please turn to page 125.*

"Cones · Sundaes · Shakes · Hotdogs · Hamburgers · Fries" reads the roofline sign of the *OX YOKE SNACK BAR*, Route 6, **GALETON**... making sure all the basics are covered. Constructed of sleek-looking large black and white glass blocks, the Ox Yoke was re-modeled to its present mod appearance in 1951. It's a good looking food stop.

In spite of its many name changes, the Frazer has been owned by one man, Sylvester Cavalati, since moved from its original location in Paoli in 1957. It's been called the Frazer Diner since 1989.

Menu design element, Crabbs Tropical Treat, Hanover

Billboard, Route 209 north, Hazleton

Founded by brothers Bernie and Harry Byorek in September, 1937, and very definitely still a **HAZLETON** institution is the ***KNOTTY PINE RESTAURANT*** (nee the Knotty Pine Drive-In), 26th and North Church Streets/Route 309. While the Knotty Pine's exterior is a handsome orange and white and plate glass, what I like most is the collection of wonderful early photographs and menus that brighten the restaurant's interior...and trace the Knotty Pine's history from a small curbside operation (Bernie Byorek had taken a trip to Florida in the mid-1930s and had been amazed at the number of curb service establishments in operation in the Sunshine State) to the present-day full-scale/full-service model.

Another Hazleton noteworthy is ***JIMMY'S QUICK LUNCH***, 123 East Broad Street. Glass brick bordered with black, an orange overhang, a green and orange awning, and a most appealing large red "Jimmy's" (with a hot dog and a roll) hanging neon sign all add up to a facade that's a visual treat.

Last, still in Hazleton, is the rather striking large red, white and blue neon sign for the otherwise all-too-modernized ***BLUE COMET DINER***, 45 South Church Street/Route 309.

Jimmy's...and its "We Will Be On Vacation" sign. A little slice of Main Street, U.S.A.

"My wife's the granddaughter; I do restoration work; and it was available." That's how 31-year old David Keller sums up the saga of the rebirth of the **HAINES SHOE HOUSE**, a unique slice of roadside architecture located on Shoe House Road (where else?) in **HELLAM** (just outside of York, off Route 462). The Shoe House was the concoction of shoe wizard Mahlon N. Haines. Starting with a $127.00 consignment of shoes in the early 1920s, Haines amassed a shoe store empire that stretched over several states and was worth millions. His secret to success: attract attention to himself - and his shoes - via flamboyant antics and spectacular advertising. The Shoe House, constructed in 1948, was his greatest achievement. Modeled after a high-topped work shoe, the House is wood frame covered with wire lath and then coated with stucco. It's definitely the large, economy size: forty-eight feet in length, seventeen feet in width, and

twenty-five feet in height.

Built as a guest house - as well as a giant advertisement for Haines' shoes - the House played gratis host to many an elderly and honeymooning couple until Mahlon Haines' death in 1962. It then served as an ice cream parlor - albeit a slowly deteriorating one - into the 1980s. In the spring of 1987 the Shoe House came back into the Haines' family when Annie Haines Keller, Mahlon's granddaughter, and her husband David purchased the almost-four-decades-old structure. Four years, over $50,000, and untold hours of toil later Annie and David have restored the Shoe House to its original lustre. It's again an ice cream parlor, with plans well along to convert part of it to a bed and breakfast. There's even to be a honeymoon suite in the cavernous toe. In fact, David reported, there's a couple from Lancaster who've been holding off their marriage until the suite is shipshape (shoeshape?).

David Keller and the miniature Shoe House that serves as a dog house. There's even a shoe-shaped sandbox on the grounds!

If a Gas Station Beautiful award were to be presented to Pennsylvania's most attractive and most lovingly maintained service station, one station certain to be in the running would be **DEAN FOWLER'S SERVICE STATION,** 1140 Main Street, **HONESDALE**. That's in no small measure due to the care of Fowler's manager, Frederick "Bus" Hartman. Now seventy-five, Bus has been on the job at Fowler's for a remarkable fifty-four years, starting there in 1936 when the station was but a year old. He recalls when the neighboring Lackawaxen River flooded up over the pumps. That was in the forties. He recalls the gas lines. That was in the seventies. And he recalls when Texaco - Fowler's has always been a Texaco outlet - wanted the station to change its lovely white-with-green-trim decor to the light brown color ("terrible brown," Bus calls it) that the company was pushing for all its stations. That was in the early eighties. Fortunately the townspeople got wind of it, came to Dean Fowler, and asked him to leave the station as is. Dean agreed. Result: the station's still white and still beautiful.

Just down the hill from the majestic Asa Packer (the railroad magnate who founded Lehigh University) mansion and right around the corner from the Hotel Switzerland (because of its magnificent mountain setting, **JIM THORPE** is known as "The Switzerland of America") sits the *SUNRISE DINER*. Originally named Steve's Diner, the Sunrise was manufactured by the Jerry O'Mahony company, and transported to Jim Thorpe in 1951. Its initial proprietor was Steve Kochmar, who'd operated a small wooden fifteen stooler, also called Steve's Diner, on the same site since 1940 or so.

Purchased by John and Susan Bartelt in 1983 (and renamed the Sunrise by them), the diner is quite lovely, with an exterior of stainless and blue, well-tended potted plants and shrubbery out front, blue curtains, and, for outdoor dining, an attached deck with picnic tables and umbrellas.

Sign above the grill at the Sunset Diner: the English may not be too good but the sentiment certainly is.

"Modest" sign adorning the CONEY ISLAND LUNCH, Clinton and Locust Streets, JOHNSTOWN.

A real trouper is the **WEST SHORE DINER**, 1011 State Street, **LEMOYNE** (1 mile E of Harrisburg). A Silk City (manufactured by the Paterson Vehicle Company, Paterson, New Jersey), the West Shore has been moved around the Harrisburg area at least four times in its approximately fifty-year lifetime. It's been at its present site since the early 1980s. While not a knockout, the West Shore has a pleasant white with maroon exterior, a comfy interior.

"Gracious" is the word that most comes to mind in trying to describe the **FENCE DRIVE-IN**, located along the shores of the west branch of the Susquehanna River on Route 405 in **MILTON**. It's a scenic location, and one that's been home to roadside fare for over fifty years. In the 1930s and 1940s there was a tent stand known as Breezy Acres. Then, in 1951-52, Bob Reitz constructed the present large wooden frame building. A local contractor, he was actually building it for someone else. But, at the last minute,

Just about the first thing you notice after you've crossed the state line into **MATAMORAS** *is the snappy-looking large round Texaco sign (the old-fashioned kind, all metal with the bright red star) that announces JOE SELNECK'S TEXACO, a quite handsome circa 1950 service station at 111 Pennsylvania Avenue/Route 6. You don't see too many of them - the good old Texaco signs - around anymore.*

the someone else got cold feet, and Reitz ended up owning and operating the place himself. The present-day proprietor, Rob Rabb, purchased it from Reitz in 1975.

With its handsome bright white - set off by green awnings - main building, its tree-shaded picnic tables overlooking the river, its potted geraniums and petunias, and its bevy of carhops (or "tablehops," if you prefer to sit at one of the picnic tables), the Fence is just plain and simply a wonderful place to enjoy a spring, summer, or fall meal.

The carhop crew in front of the Fence:
"Don't Drive By! Give The Fence A Try!"

151

Original Paramount Diners' clock,
Vale-Rio Diner

The *VALE-RIO DINER* - "The Bright Spot of Phoenixville," reads the menu - came to Nutt Road in **PHOENIXVILLE** on Thanksgiving Day, 1948. It opened for business that very night. A Paramount (built by Paramount Diners, Haledon, New Jersey), the Vale-Rio is a large all-stainless with glass brick rounded corners model, decorated with what I think of as "record disc" design (although I'm sure Paramount had a more exotic name for it!). The interior of the diner (which takes its name from initial proprietors Pat and Charles Valerio) is an alluring pink, burgundy, and gray, and features a still-working Paramount clock above the entrance to the kitchen.

In the early 1940s, Levengood Dairies, then a prospering Pottstown dairy, erected three milk and ice cream retail outlets (one in Pottstown, one in Boyertown, and one in Pennsburg) that were shaped like a cup. We are fortunate to yet have all three in existence. Originally just a cup-shaped structure made of heavy-guage steel with sliding doors through which patrons were served, all three have been added onto. But the cup is still there in each structure, the clearly visable focal point. All are today full-scale eat-in establishments: *THE CUP*, 903 North Charlotte Street, **POTTSTOWN**: *THE NORTH END SANDWICH SHOP*, 237 North Reading Avenue, **BOYERTOWN**: and *THE PENN CUP*, Jackson Street and Pottstown Avenue, **PENNSURG**.

The Cup: A Pottstown favorite for close to fifty years.

Elegantly set amidst Victorian townhouses is the *GARFIELD DINER*, Garfield Square/West Market Street, **POTTSVILLE.** A Kullman (manufactured by the Kullman Dining Car Company, Harrison, New Jersey), the Garfield has had but two owners in its thirty-six years of existence: Thomas Joulwan from 1954 to 1970, and Joseph Thomas from 1970 until the present. Be sure to ask for Kathy Christ, a waitress who's been on duty at the Garfield since opening day in 1954. She can tell you everything you might ever want to know about the diner, including the day it was delivered (she watched it being set up August 23, 1954); when JFK posed for photos on the diner's steps after making a speech in Pottsville in 1960; about the motorcycle gang that used to frequent the Garfield (and would chase the cook around if they didn't feel their meal was up to snuff). "I could write a book about this place," Kathy told me. I believe she could. (Note: for a look at the Garfield on a day when it must've seemed as if just about everybody in the state were there, please turn to page 61.).

Since 1926 the **CORNER LUNCH**, so named because of its location on the corner of Indiana and Gilpen Streets, <u>PUNXSUTAWNEY</u>, has been serving up hot dogs, hamburgs, and sandwiches. What makes the Corner Lunch special is its unique layout: it's shaped like a triangle in order to make optimum use of its corner space. The Corner (a.k.a. Carlino's, in honor of proprietor George Carlino) is also intimate (translate "small": it's a seven stooler), which only adds to its charm.

One of my favorite finds in all of Pennsylvania was this marvelous Punxsutawney Phil wall mural that so brightens the city's downtown. Measuring forty feet in length by fifteen feet in height, it was designed by Marie Hensley of the Art III class at Punxsutawney Area High School and painted by she and five of her classmates in October, 1982. Does Phil look resplendent in his bright red bow tie and black top hat? You bet he does!

Sign, Route 30 west, <u>SADSBURY-VILLE</u> (20 miles E of Lancaster)

153

What Greek immigrant Pete Gorant began back in 1918 is still wondrously with us in the magic of the *CONEY ISLAND LUNCH*, 218 East Independent Street, <u>SHAMOKIN</u>. To step inside its door is to be transformed - well, to be *almost* transformed - to a time of long ago. There's the white marble counter; thirteen (no superstition here) metal swivel stools; hanging globe lamps; marble-topped tables; copper coffee urn hood; and twenty-two foot high pressed-tin ceiling. All are original!

The Coney Island is today owned by Helen Grant, Pete Gorant's daughter. Its bill of fare consists of five items: hot dogs, hamburgers, coffee, milk, and soda (served in painted label bottles from Reichert's Beverages of nearby Treverton). And that's it. So go and enjoy a hot dog or a hamburger or a bottle of good local soda pop. But go. The Coney Island is truly a treasure!

Also in Shamokin, several blocks from the Coney Island, is the *ECONOMY SERVICE STATION*, Market and Walnut Streets. A circa 1925 white cementblock and green brick building with a wonderfully-maintained portico (with pressed-tin roof, no less!), the Economy is a tribute to filling station design. Proprietors John R. and Kathy Brennan can be proud.

How to describe the *PARK RESTAURANT*, Washington and Main Streets, <u>SHENANDOAH</u>? It's not a diner, yet it feels like one. Built circa 1940 and clad in striking lime green metal panels, it occupies a commanding position on a knoll at the head of Main Street; more or less serves as the entrance to the borough's Girard Park.

The sign that beckons, and Coney Island employees Sharon Wichurowski, left, and Lucille Lummaw. Lucille has thirty years of experience, while Sharon is the self-described new kid on the block with fifteen years under her belt. Both laughed as they told me that, to both Coney Island employees and patrons alike, a hot dog has always been known as an "up," while a hamburger has always been known as a "down." Both laughed even more as they recounted the time an unknowing customer came in and ordered 7-Up. He got it: seven hot dogs. Was he ever surprised!

The *SMETHPORT DINER*, 19 Main Street, **SMETHPORT** (15 miles SE of Bradford), is not a visual gem. Yet there is something I like about it. Maybe it's the cozy white and baby blue interior. Maybe it's the lighted white candle in each front window. Maybe it's because it's the home of the "Hubber Burger." Whatever, it's well worth a stop (and, of course, a Hubber Burger: a half-pounder surrounded with lettuce, tomatoes, onions, bacon, and, if you're really in the mood, cheese.).

Now owned by Jim and Joanie Snyder, the Smethport dates from 1933. The "Hubber Burger" - of more recent vintage - takes its name from the nickname for Smethport High's athletic teams... the Hubbers (which, in turn, comes from the fact that Smethport is McKean County's county seat...the "hub," as it were.).

Somebody goofed: when the diner's recent matchbook order arrived it was discovered that "burger" had somehow become "buger." Doesn't sound quite as appetizing, does it?

Go ahead... squeeze on in.

Wedged between two considerably larger buildings in the heart of downtown **SUNBURY** is the adorable - and aptly named - *SQUEEZE-IN*. Six feet wide by eighteen feet deep, the Squeeze-In holds a grill and five stools and not much more. To just get in the door takes a fair amount of shifting on the part of those already inside. A lunch counter since turn-of-the-century days, the eatery was known as Snyder's Lunch until 1945 when Thelma Sterling purchased it and coined the Squeeze-In name. Today, forty-five years later, it's still the Squeeze-In and it's still in the Sterling family: Thelma's son Sam is the proud proprietor. The minuscule establishment's specialty is - of course - a Squeezeburger (a pair of hamburger patties with cheese in the middle and topped with mustard, relish, onions, and/or catsup). If you're in Sunbury, stop by, squeeze in, and enjoy one.

*A peek, circa 1948, at the Wellsboro
Diner when it was known as Schanaker's.*

Highlighting **WELLSBORO**'s handsome Main Street is the ***WELLSBORO DINER***, 19 Main Street/ Routes 6 and 287, one of the classiest diners/ dinors I found in my wanderings around the Commonwealth. Opened in April of 1939, the Wellsboro is a Sterling Diner (manufactured in Merrimac, Massachusetts) that started out, on the same site, as Schanaker's Diner. It was initially owned by brothers-in-law Loui Meier and Walter Schanaker. But not for long: in 1940 Loui bought Walter out (although the name "Schanaker" stuck until well into the sixties). In 1967 Clem and Kay Sipe became the new owners. Since 1972 it's been Doratha and Roy Cummings. Each, it's apparent, has taken great pride in the diner. From its interior yellow barrel roof, lovely wood exhaust grills, and glass-topped counter to its exterior of yellow and green porcelainized metal, the Wellsboro looks almost as if it could've been wheeled in from Merrimac yesterday. If you're traveling across the top of the state you won't want to miss it.

The diner today, and Doratha Cummings, on the right, with her star cook and twenty-two year veteran, Thelma, on the left. "Fastest short-order cook in the east," Doratha boasts of Thelma. It's quite a billing.

Thelma in action.

Present-day Delights

Present-day sign ornamentation, Jerry's Curb Service.

Jerry's Curb Service as it appeared in 1948. That's Jerry's snappy-looking Ford convertible sitting out front.

Don't try finding **WEST BRIDGE-WATER** on the map. It isn't there. But, no matter. Everybody, it seems, in the Beaver/Beaver Falls/New Brighton area west of Pittsburgh knows where **JERRY'S CURB SERVICE** is. Jerry's is an institution. As is so often the case, however, it's an institution that happened more or less by accident. It was early 1947. Twenty-year old Jerry Reed's stint in the Air Force was over. Jerry had been stationed in Denver and loved it. But he couldn't find a job. So, reluctantly, the Beaver native started home. On the way he, in his own words, "went flat broke" in Fort Wayne, Indiana. There he discovered the drive-in restaurant: "There was a curb service place...everybody hangin' out and having fun."

It took a few months but Jerry eventually made it back to western Pennsylvania. Once there he set out to

open his own curb service restaurant. People around the area told him it wouldn't work - "People won't eat in their cars." - but Jerry persisted. On September 29th of that same year, 1947, Jerry's Curb Service opened, the first carhop operation in the Pennsyl-

vania/Ohio/West Virginia tri-states region. Forty-three years - and five crushing floods - later, Jerry's is still going strong. Located just off Route 51, Jerry's is open all year. If you're in the neighborhood you won't want to miss it.

Carhop Orpha "Tunie" Smith serves a "Famous Jerry's Cheeseburger" to customer Bob Zanker. Tunie has been carhopping at Jerry's since 1967...close to a quarter of a century! If that doesn't make her the longest reigning carhop in the country it sure puts her right up there near the top of the list.

Green and white and stainless steel meld together very nicely at the **D-K DINER**, 609 East Gay Street, **WEST CHESTER**. Owned by Gus Correa since January of 1987, the D-K is a 1947 Mountain View (manufactured by Mountain View Diners, Singac, New Jersey). The "D-K" comes from the last names of the two families that initially owned it, Davis and Kappe.

The D-K's exterior is a most becoming stainless with green horizontal stripes, a green and white awning, and what almost appears to be a white picket fence embellishing the roofline. The interior also features stainless with a healthy dose of green. What impressed me most, though, is how well-maintained everything appears to be. It could almost be 1947 all over again.

The D-K team: Gus with his waitresses - and his nieces - Sandra and Adrianna Correa.

A second diner in West Chester, on Route 202 south, is the **BIRMINGHAM GRILL**, a somewhat rough and ready large circa 1945 Kullman (Kullman Dining Car Co., Harrison, New Jersey) that features glass block rounded corners, and a stainless and blue exterior and interior. A real trucker's favorite, you may have difficulty spotting the diner for all the trucks parked out front and all around.

Last, just before you're out of West Chester, is **JIMMY JOHN'S PIPIN' HOT**. Located about a mile further south on Route 202 than the Birmingham Grill, Jimmy John's goes back to 1940. This is its third building, dating to 1960. It's noteworthy largely because of the tremendous collection of through-the-years' snapshots that adorn, almost like wallpaper, a vast share of the Pipin' Hot's wall space. There are a good three-hundred from the early 1940s alone: sort of a roll call of the eatery's early patrons.

A trio of Wilkes-Barre's best: left, the Olympic Diner; above, the Chow Tyme; below, a side view of Palooka's.

PALOOKA'S DINER, East Market Street and Wilkes-Barre Boulevard, **WILKES-BARRE**, is named in tribute to Ham Fisher, the Wyoming Valley native who created the Joe Palooka comic strip. It's a Mountain View (manufactured by Mountain View Diners, Singac, New Jersey) that was moved to its present site - across from the massively beautiful former Stegmaier brewery - from nearby Exeter in 1986. And it's definitely trendy: pink and black decor, old Coke machine, old Coke signs, attached Budd railroad dining car, etc. As the notation on the menu reads: "All hula hoops and poodle skirts must be checked in at the door."

Far less trendy Wilkes-Barre silver queens are the ***OLYMPIC DINER*** (the former Handley's Diner), a large Paramount (Paramount Diners, Haledon, New Jersey) that's located at Dana and South Main Streets, and the ***CHOW TYME DINER***, a Jerry O'Mahony (Jerry O'Mahony company, Elizabeth, New Jersey) model that brightens the 500 block of Blackman Street.

If you like blue, you'll love ***LEE'S DINER***, 4320 West Market Street/Route 30, **YORK**. The outside only hints of blue (there are blue Venetian blinds that show through the windows): it's mostly stainless with bands of red. But the inside is true blue: blue (and tan) roof, blue (and tan) floor, blue booths, blue stools, and, of course, the blue Venetian blinds again. Built in the early 1950s by Mountain View Diners, Singac, New Jersey, Lee's still has its grill out front, affording patrons a view of all the happenings.

THE END

PHOTOGRAPH/GRAPHIC CREDITS

Page	Description	Courtesy
VIII	Kendall Tourist Camp Postcard	Al Matthews, Nottingham, N.H.
4	Extra Bite Wheel Cafe photograph	Potsdam Public Museum, Potsdam, N.Y.
6	White House Cafe photograph	Worcester Historical Museum, Worcester, Mass.
7	T.H. Buckley advertisements	Worcester Historical Museum, Worcester, Mass.
10	Tops Diner postcard	Iris Nevins, Sussex, N.J.
10	Grand Diner postcard	The Hug Collection, Lorain, Ohio
27	Marbett's photograph	Tombrock Corp., Stamford, Conn.
28	Hot Shoppe photographs	Library of Congress, Washington, D.C.
31	*Life* cover	Francis Miller, *Life* Magazine, c. Time Warner, Inc.
32	First drive-in theatre, Camden	The Historical Society of Pennsylvania, Philadelphia, Pa.
37	Drive-in theatre photograph	Standard Oil Collection, Univ. of Louisville Photographic Archives, Louisville, Ky.
42	White Tower photographs	Library of Congress, Washington, D.C.
47	McDonald's photograph	Broome County Historical Society, Binghamton, N.Y.
51	Boy and gas pump photograph	Joseph Basher, Lancaster, N.Y.
52	Brooker's Maple Shade photograph	North Castle Historical Society, Armonk, N.Y.
52	Centennial Diner postcard	The Hug Collection, Lorain, Ohio
53	Cloister Diner postcard	The Hug Collection, Lorain, Ohio
54	The Coffee Pot	Library of Congress, Washington, D.C.
54	Colonial Diner photograph	Standard Oil Collection, Univ. of Louisville Photographic Archives, Louisville, Ky.
55	Crew Levick photograph	Lehigh County Historical Society, Allentown, Pa.
56	The Igloo photograph	Fred Arone, Dobbs Ferry, N.Y.
56	Dave Baird Texaco photograph	Joseph G. Streamer, Hamburg Town Historian, Hamburg, N.Y.
57	Dave's Dream postcard	The Hug Collection, Lorain, Ohio
58	Ebby's Diner photograph	Library of Congress, Washington, D.C.
59	Ed's Diner postcard	The Hug Collection, Lorain, Ohio
59	Elm & Maiden Lane photograph	Yates County Historical Society, Penn Yan, N.Y.
60	4th Street Diner photograph	Library of Congress, Washington, D.C.
60	Frank's Tydol photograph	Municipal Archives, City of New York
61	JFK/Garfield Diner photographs	The Historical Society of Schuylkill County, Pottsville, Pa.
63	Grand View Point postcards	The Hug Collection, Lorain, Ohio
64	Gus' Michigan Red Hots	Gus'/Print Pad, Ltd., Plattsburgh, N.Y.
65	Black Cat postcard	The Hug Collection, Lorain, Ohio
67	Golden Arrow Diner postcard	The Hug Collection, Lorain, Ohio
70	Rhinebeck Diner postcard	Iris Nevins, Sussex, N.J.
72	Texaco Grill/Woodworth's Restaurant	The Hug Collection, Lorain, Ohio
72	Trent Diner postcard	The Hug Collection, Lorain, Ohio
74	Howard Johnson's photograph	Standard Oil Collection, Univ. of Louisville Photograhic Archives, Louisville, Ky.
75	Jack's Lunch photograph	Charles L. Radzinsky, Middletown, N.Y.
75	Jim & Bill's Mari-Nay Diner postcard	The Hug Collection, Lorain, Ohio
76	Lawrence Tourist Cabins' postcard	The Hug Collection, Lorain, Ohio
78	Minnich's Gulf Station photograph	Cumberland County Historical Society, Carlisle, Pa.
78	Three friends' photograph	Resource and Research Center For Beaver County, Beaver Falls, Pa.
79	Penn State Flyer billboard	Standard Oil Collection, Univ. of Louisville Photographic Archives, Louisville, Ky.
80	Phil & Ernie's Service Station	Municipal Archives, City of New York
81	The Pig Stand photographs	Williard B. Williams, Camillus, N.Y.
83	Richfield/Richlube station	Cortland County Historical Society, Cortland, N.Y.
83	Rice's Diner photograph	DeWitt Historical Society of Tompkins County, Ithaca, N.Y.
84	Riverside Diner photograph	Library of Congress, Washington, D.C.
85	Sheeler's Garage photograph	Chester County Historical Society, West Chester, Pa.
86	Sky-Way Drive-In photograph	Erie County Historical Society, Erie, Pa.
86	Sterling Diners matchbook cover	The Hug Collection, Lorain, Ohio
87	Sunset Diner billboard	Standard Oil Collection, Univ. of Louisville Photographic Archives, Louisville, Ky.
90	Walt's Restaurant photograph	Standard Oil Collection, Univ. of Louisville Photographic Archives, Louisville, Ky.
91	Westchester Diner photograph	Fred Arone, Dobbs Ferry, N.Y.
92-93	White Tower photographs	Tombrock Corp., Stamford, Conn.
116	Heid's circa 1954 photograph	Helen Heid Platner, Heid's, Liverpool, N.Y.
118	Walter's 1931 photograph	Gene Warrington, Walter's, Mamaroneck, N.Y.
130	Silver Lake Drive-In material	Rick Stefanon, Silver Lake Drive-In Theatre, Perry, N.Y.
156	Schanaker's photograph	Doratha Cummings, Wellsboro Diner, Wellsboro, Pa.
158	Jerry's Curb Service, 1948	Jerry Reed, Jerry's Curb Service, West Bridgewater, Pa.

All graphic material not listed above is from the author's collection.

Index